35.00

LISTENING TO MUSIC

1995. 3. 10. ~~the~~ Zwemmer,
Charing Cross Road, London

SWANSEA STUDIES IN PHILOSOPHY

General Editor: D.Z. Phillips, Professor of Philosophy, University College of Swansea

Philosophy is the struggle for clarity about the contexts of human discourse we engage in. What we need is not theoretical explanation, but clarification and elucidation of what lies before us. Recent returns to theory in many fields of philosophy, involving more and more convoluted attempts to meet inevitable counter-examples to such theories, make this need all the more urgent. This series affords an opportunity for writers who share this conviction, one as relevant to logic, epistemology and the philosophy of mind, as it is to ethics, politics, aesthetics and the philosophy of religion. Authors will be expected to engage with the thought of influential philosophers and contemporary movements, thus making the series a focal point for lively discussion.

R.W. Beardsmore
ETHICS SINCE 1950

David Cockburn
OTHER HUMAN BEINGS

John Edelman
AN AUDIENCE FOR MORAL PHILOSOPHY?

Martyn Evans
LISTENING TO MUSIC

Raimond Gaita
GOOD AND EVIL: AN ABSOLUTE CONCEPTION

D.Z. Phillips
INTERVENTIONS IN ETHICS

WITTGENSTEIN AND RELIGION

B.R. Tilghman
WITTGENSTEIN, ETHICS AND AESTHETICS: THE VIEW FROM
    ETERNITY

Listening to Music

Martyn Evans

University College Fellow
Centre for Philosophy and Health Care
University College of Swansea, Wales

MACMILLAN

First published 1990

Published by
THE MACMILLAN PRESS LTD
Houndmills, Basingstoke, Hampshire RG21 2XS
and London
Companies and representatives
throughout the world

Filmset by
Wearside Tradespools,
Fulwell, Sunderland

Printed in Hong Kong

British Library Cataloguing in Publication Data
Evans, Martyn, 1956–
    Listening to music. – (Swansea studies in philosophy).
    1. Music. Appreciation. Cultural aspects
    I. Title   II. Series
    780'.1'5
    ISBN 0–333–52990–1

For my mother and father, who encouraged in me a love of
music and of learning

Contents

Acknowledgements

This is not a work of textual scholarship, nor an exercise in specifically Wittgensteinian philosophy, but the influence of Wittgenstein will be readily apparent in what follows. His thoughts were my springboard, and in a sense they are also my goal.

Throughout the preparation of this essay I have been helped and encouraged by my family and by my friends, and to them I owe a debt of thanks. I am very grateful also to Shirley Wollen who typed the script and who made many helpful suggestions as to its format, and to my wife Janet, who patiently read the proofs.

Some of the ideas I develop here have been listened to by members of the Philosophical Society at University College, Cardiff, among them Professor J. L. Evans and members of the academic staff of the Department of Philosophy; their criticisms and responses have helped me enormously. In the same manner, I have benefited greatly from discussions with Professor D. Z. Phillips of University College, Swansea. I am indebted also to Dr Robert Sharpe of St David's University College, Lampeter, both for extremely helpful and stimulating discussions, and for giving me the opportunity to air a synoptic version of the argument to the Philosophical Society at Lampeter. However, my greatest debt is to my friend and colleague, Dr Donald Evans of University College, Swansea, who first interested me in philosophy, cultivated and directed that interest, guided me in the choice of my area of study and steered me past the worst of the pitfalls that awaited me. His insight and sheer enthusiasm have made this essay possible.

It is customary at this point for writers to admit that since they have received so much help, it is the errors which remain that are their own. Unfortunately in my case this happens to be true.

1
A Tale of Two Listeners

Walk into the music section of any decent library and select, in as aimless a way as you like, a dozen or so books about things like composition, the lives of the acknowledged masters, the rudiments of analysis, the history of specific forms and styles, the niceties of interpretation and so on. Read through them at random and pictures will begin to emerge of the experience of listening to music. Not, of course, that the writers need set out consciously to draw such pictures. Nor need their opening remarks lay down the fundamentals of musical experience. Rather, the beliefs they hold about listening will percolate through what they actually say. Whatever their conscious enterprise, they will have assumptions and presuppositions about listening which will inform their discussion. For, after all, it seems likely that it is their own listening which has motivated and indeed which perhaps largely constitutes their particular studies. To discourse, for instance, on a particular composer or on a particular style, or to elaborate on a theory of expression or of musical symbolism they will have listened intensively and extensively. And their own listening may have been of a very methodical and considered kind. The nature of listening is important to their field of interest.

Having said this, hardly any of the books of musicology, style, textual criticism or reviews of the repertoire pay much conscious attention to the listener, to his attitudes or to his qualifications. Yet they all make certain large assumptions, and these assumptions are quite as revealing as openly psychological or philosophical forays into musical aesthetics, where, as is too often the case, the nature of musical experience figures so prominently as to be in danger of shrivelling beyond recognition under the intensity of artificial lighting.

There is a rather odd book, *Music Today*, written in 1934 by one John Foulds, who, in the course of setting out an avowedly occult aesthetic full of astral planes and Buddhic symbolism, makes an observation about the sort of language in which most reflections on music are written. I think it is worth noticing:

1

The voluminous labours of aestheticians in the world of music are usually expressed in one or other of two ways: either in dry technical terms or in the language of poetic fiction. That their conclusions are distressingly nebulous may be not altogether unexpected from the nature of the subject: that they should in almost every case fail to mention one of the facts of outstanding importance to musicians and non-musicians alike is however surprising.[1]

Promising though the 'important fact' sounds, it turns out to be quite as nebulous as the conclusions of the aestheticians who have so upset Foulds, and I don't propose to pursue it. But that the vast bulk of writing on music does indeed consist, as Foulds claims, of a mixture of technical language (often dry) and figurative expressions (often perplexing) is undeniable. But anyone who tries – as I shall – to give a philosophical account of the position of the listener must start from these raw data. The moment that anyone begins to say what music in general or some piece of music in particular is, or 'is about', he starts to use either technical phrases like 'invertible subject', figurative terms like 'incandescent radiance' or mystical ones like 'spirituality'. An account of the experience of listening must start with the sorts of things to which listening gives rise or in which listening is expressed – principally, the judgements made by those who listen about what they are listening to. And clearly the most widely available of these are the judgements of those whose listening is important (or lucrative) enough to propel pen to paper.

Let me say at once that the technical vocabulary of musical discourse is so well established, documented and explored that even were I able to examine it in anything like a scholarly fashion (which I am not) I should not propose to do so. It seems unlikely that we could infer anything about the prerequisites underlying the listener merely by elaborating in further detail upon the ramifications of technical analysis. On the other hand, there is not – nor could be – any systematic account of the meaning of verbal images, metaphors and figurative or poetic language more generally. That is not the sort of thing poetic language is. And as for the links between the two kinds of language, technical and poetic, if analytic descriptions alone of a particular piece of music could yield the images which are subsequently deployed towards it then the production of images would be an exact science, which it is not. Whereas if images could yield technical accounts, then disputes of interpretation could always be sorted out by looking up the rudiments of music, which, alas, they cannot.

What we have to do, then, is to look at the way judgements about music are used, and then look through those judgements at the concepts, faculties and attitudes which they presuppose, at the activities underlying the judgements. We need to look at the picture of the listener which they generate. To start with let us make a short, cursory and haphazard sortie into some examples of critical writing and see what sort of a picture emerges.

Here is composer, arranger and theoretician Ferruccio Busoni:

> To music indeed it is given to set in vibration our human moods: Dread (*Leporello*), oppression of soul, invigoration, lassitude (Beethoven's last quartets), decision (*Wotan*), hesitation, despondency, encouragement, harshness, tenderness, excitement, tranquillisation ... likewise the inner echo of external occurrences which is bound up in the moods of the soul. But not the moving cause itself of these spiritual affections. . . .²

Clearly Busoni thinks that music stimulates the emotions, but by other means than simply reproducing the familiar mechanical causes of emotion. The listener has his human moods 'set in vibrations'. Presumably he can distinguish these moods from those brought on by workaday 'moving causes'. But this is a rather ambiguous picture of our listener. Is he a willing accessory, and if so, why? Why submit to those emotions ordinarily avoided – fear, horror, grief and so on? Or are these not really part of the repertoire? Furthermore, what qualifies him to feel them purely on account of an aural phenomenon? Is it a question of instinct or of learning, of an applied stimulus or of the exercise of his will and imagination? Perhaps indeed emotion might be merely a welcome by-product of listening. And sometimes it might be distinctly unwelcome. Alternatively it might, as Busoni seems to think, be the central purpose of music. But here the exact nature of the musical vehicle might be peripheral – and I cannot imagine Busoni admitting *this*. Clearly then there are large assumptions behind a piece of writing which many people might take at first sight to be self-evident. It is worth pointing out that since Busoni cites certain named works in connection with particular moods (*Wotan*, the last quartets) he must think that particular musical effects are predictable and repeatable. This might be true but it could have a psychological rather than an aesthetic explanation. To decide, we need to know more.

One way of conjuring up moods is through specific program-mes, depicting real or imagined scenes and events, and much music is deployed to this end. The question then arises of how central such a purpose might be. The critic Robert Layton discusses Sibelius's symphonic poem *Tapiola*:

> One does not have to have experienced the vast forests of Scandinavia with all their variety of moods, colours and sounds, their immense loneliness, their magic and terror for Sibelius' *Tapiola* to make its impact. Its greatness communicates itself independently of its extra-musical intentions. Although it is as perfect an evocation of the forest as *La Mer* is of the sea, its greatness lies in its impact in terms of pure music.[3]

Several questions lie beneath the surface here – what is pure, and what alloyed music? And if the extra-musical programme is not essential to the music's impact as 'great', what possible importance could it have at all? Is it perhaps a way into the music for apprentice listeners, to be discarded on graduation day? Well, this seems plausible but if true it leans heavily towards one particular picture of listening as a developing *skill*. Again, we can imagine one listener having his actual experience of the Finnish forest as it were replayed or fulfilled for him in the sounds of the music; another might use the music as a stimulus to his imagining what such a forest might be like; and yet a third – such as, apparently, Layton himself – by-passing the programme altogether and going straight to the musical structures and its timbres, seeking and finding satisfaction there. Now maybe 'seeking' is the operative word here. In the variety of possible approaches (leaving aside for the moment questions about which, if any, are the more legitimate) the listener seems to be deliberately out to get something. He wants to get a picture or an impression of the forest, or alternative-ly, he wants to get past all that to the 'pure music' itself. Now, is a search for any visual association idiosyncratic, extrinsic to the music? Sibelius's very titling of the symphonic poem suggests that that cannot be entirely true. Yet the conclusion of Layton's approach would appear to be that we don't really need the title and its associated images in the last analysis. Furthermore, if we did need them, might not the title end up doing most of the work? Or could just any imaginative programme be read into the music, provided it were satisfying and fulfilling to the listener? The remarkable and powerful couplings of music with film images, so well explored, for instance, in Kubrick's *2001* and in many films since, suggest limitless possibilities in this area. But this raises awkward questions about the intentions of the composer. And then we have to ask whether a particular piece of music really provides one visual programme in a uniquely immediate way. If this were true of *Tapiola*, for instance, then Layton would appear to be standing at a distance from the music in his appreciation of its impact as 'pure music'. That sounds rather like a decision he would have had to take consciously. But of course that could apply equally to hearing the programme itself.

Such decisions may well be partly definitive of the listener; listening is, after all, to be distinguished from merely hearing. Even to identify a piece of music as 'serious' rather than as 'light' seems to involve outlining a particular context within which the music must be heard. Now Ferruccio Busoni ends up throwing the burden of explaining this context on the apparently cosmic nature of music as a kind of ideal entity, or perhaps a *ding-an-sich*. Having suggested, as we saw above, that music sets in vibration the moods of the soul without reference to gross external causes, he continues:

> Is it possible to imagine how a poor, contented man could be represented by music? The contentment, the soul state, can be interpreted by music; but where does the poverty appear, or the important ethic problem stated in the words 'poor, but contented'? This is due to the fact that 'poor' connotes a phase of terrestrial and social conditions not to be found in the eternal harmony. And music is a part of the vibrating universe.[4]

From this, whatever the limitations on its representational properties, music seems to have a kind of elevated, guaranteed existence regardless of any particular context which we might ordinarily think of as characteristically 'expressive' or 'aesthetic'. So perhaps the listening attitude consists in setting aside, for a time, 'terrestrial and social conditions' and turning our attention to the eternal harmony of the 'vibrating universe'. We turn away from the mundane to the sublime. Well, it is an attractive thought, and fairly popular on that account; but like all attractive thoughts it needs careful scrutiny. On this view music would seem to have nothing to do with ordinary life, offering instead a glimpse of some higher alternative; but this seems to rule out at a stroke all programmatic music. And an examination of our moods and feelings might reveal that they are necessarily directed towards mundane situations. What price *Wotan* now on the strength of this part of Busoni's account? Anyway, even if Busoni is right, on what basis does the listener direct his attention away from the mundane and towards the sublime? Is it instinctual – does it need merely a trigger of some sort? Or is it the product of a self-conscious and deliberate discipline?

These questions, together with the question of the spontaneity of the visual programme of, say, the Scandinavian forest, raise two alternative views of the listener. On the one hand the listener is engaged in decisions, imposing images on the music. Alternatively the music imposes the images on the listener. And which we choose will have implications for the kind of activity that we think listening is. This account of a recital given by Liszt could support either view:

> By leaving the organisations of his concerts to others, Liszt sometimes fell victim to amusing errors. He once played in Marseilles, and included in the programme his arrangements of Schubert's *La Truite* ('The Trout'). Owing to a printing error the piece appeared as *La Trinité* and the unsuspecting audience sat through this bubbling music with quasi-religious reverence. When Liszt realised the mistake he got up from the piano and made an impromptu speech, asking the audience not to confuse the mysterious idea of the Trinity with Schubert's trout, a helpful interjection which caused great hilarity.[5]

Now the fact that the audience laughed suggests that the incongruity was real enough, but the fact that they laughed only *after* the explanation had been given to them by the luckless Liszt makes it unclear where the incongruity should be located – in their enterprising determination to impose a religious programme on whatever they heard, no matter how unlikely, or in their politeness in indulging Liszt whilst he played on unaware of the blunder? Did they twig that something was amiss before Liszt did? In other words, as we think of this particular audience, was the jollity of the exuberant trout a feature of the music, or merely of the approach of a suitably primed listener? What would they have heard had they known? And what *did* they hear under their corporate illusion? Are we as listeners responsive to the presented sounds, or are we obedient to a title or to a programme note? The interesting thing about Liszt's nightmare is that when the presented sounds were separated from their verbal rationale, the audience was unsure which to follow. And that really means that they did not know which was primary. It would be interesting to play this same deception on a modern audience. Perhaps indeed some modern composers do this all the time. At any rate, the question of whether the images are imposed upon the music by the listener, or upon the listener by the music, is a real one. Does the listener approach the work, or does he sit back and wait for it to approach him?

This could be partly settled by asking whether a particular response is a general one or whether it is peculiar to a particular individual. If the former, then superficially at least it might be thought to be a product of the music – always assuming that the listeners had not been primed by the title or by loaded biographical notes and so on. Whereas an idiosyncratic response would look, superficially, like the action of one person's imagination on the sounds that he heard. Unfortunately it is not as simple as that. For we need to know something about the qualifications of the listeners involved. Indeed, this much is implied in our caveat concerning an audience's biographical assumptions about the composer's intentions. And that kind of caution opens up the whole question of whether it even makes sense to ask for a listener to approach a work in a totally innocent way, free from all preconceptions. It would be better to ask whether the listener had any preconceptions that were inappropriate to the music. But how do we decide which conceptions are appropriate, and which inappropriate? To appeal to either the title or the composer's intentions is, of course, to beg the very questions at issue.

Perhaps one way out would be to look at a particular judgement, and, without troubling ourselves over whether or not it is a minority opinion, simply ask how plausible it is. But before we consider an example, let us ask what 'plausible' is to mean. Ideally, it should mean 'true'; ideally, then, we should try to find out whether a judgement is or is not true. If true, the response would be valid; if false, a product of psychological idiosyncrasy. Unfortunately, only technical judgements could be true or false, and then only in a rather extended sense. Clearly poetic or figurative judgements are not like this. And of course there are those who doubt as a result whether figurative judgements have any meaning at all; others, more cautiously, wonder whether figurative judgements can ever be more than subjective fancy. Consider this from Donald Francis Tovey:

> It is not surprising that Bach came to think it a mistake to include the *Incarnatus* as a mere final section of this duet (i.e. from the *Credo*). This mistake he promptly repaired (in the B minor Mass) by setting this central doctrine to a chorus which, for simplicity, depth and mystery cannot be surpassed.... A violin figure hovers like the Spirit of God moving on the face of the waters, while the orchestral bass throbs slowly and the voices work out a symmetrical movement on imitative sequences of a simple chord-theme, the bottom note of which is often quite other than what we would expect.[6]

And this, also on a piece by Bach (the A minor Fugue from Book I of the *Well-Tempered Clavier*) offered by the critic Wilfrid Mellers:

> The passage is at once exciting and frightening. The last two bars, returning to the diminished segment of the theme and its thrusting trills, dam the flood as though by a conscious act of will, and with an almost triumphant foot-stamping.[7]

Both these passages combine technical and figurative language. Now we can check up in any book on musical theory on whether 'imitative sequences of a simple chord theme' or 'diminished segment' are being used properly. But 'the Spirit of God moving on the face of the waters' is rather more difficult. So is 'thrusting trills', 'dam the flood' and 'triumphant foot-stamping'. Of course, the fact that we cannot give conditions for the truth of judgements applying these expressions doesn't prevent our saying that we know perfectly well what Tovey and Mellers mean. The trouble is that in the absence of truth conditions we have yet to explain the phrase 'knowing what they mean'. *How* do we know? What does this knowing amount to? On what is it based? Yet of course a considerable part of our listening to and understanding music consists in knowing what people do mean when they say this sort of thing. Poetic language is integral to talking about music, and it is integral to the activity of listening. To be able to say much at all about the listener we have to be able to say something about this sort of language. If it really is no more than a kind of psychological *rapport* between a small group of people, listening under circumstances of heightened sensitivity in the highly charged atmosphere of the recital room – where emotions may be generated by the sheer nervous tension of live performance – then we need to be clear about it. Or if this language is the result of some mysterious action on the consciousness of the listeners by the agency of the music, then we need to be clear about that. To judge by the inaccessibility of some metaphors, this latter would often be a very tempting line to take: 'Horowitz has the genius to ravish the piano, yet leave it chaste'[8] was inspired under the circumstances of a live performance, in which the agency of the music might have worked very powerfully indeed on the vulnerable imagination of the listener; but of course as a professional critic, Neville Cardus would have been less vulnerable in this sense than most. If there is an explanation for this remark we should need to work quite hard to give it – we should need to describe a rather curious and sophisticated context in which it could make sense. The alternative is, of course, that Cardus is merely talking some private language, comprehensible perhaps only to one or two people who know him really well. But this would scarcely be legitimate criticism; we should frown on it rather as the bridge world frowns on the 'psychic bidding' of established partners: it isn't fair. Now it remains true that, if we knew more, the remark might tell us a good deal about the circumstances and assumptions underlying Cardus's listening. But properly to understand and to locate those assumptions we need already to have begun to build up our picture of the listener. And we need to be clear about the relation in which he stands to what he hears.

The question of the division of labour between the music and the listener comes up again in Erwin Doernberg's sideswipe at Hanslick, that critic who, paradoxically, was first responsible for the revolt against the domination of aesthetics by Romantic conceptions of emotion: '. . . whenever Hanslick failed to enjoy and to understand a work of music – and this happened not infrequently – he would put the blame on the composer'.[9] And why not – unless the listener himself has some sort of responsibility towards the music, which is clearly the assumption behind Doernberg's charge. But if this is so, can *any* hostility towards a piece of music be justified? Does the music – or perhaps the composer – have any responsibility towards the listener? Liszt thought so; indeed he thought there might be more than one kind:

> Art, true art, catches a chill in splendid apartments hung with red damask, and swoons away completely in *salons* of pale yellow or shimmering blue.... When at court, keep it short: what you actually say matters little, provided that the rhythm gets into their toes and makes them think of yesterday's or tomorrow's waltz![10]

Tartly put, considering that this is the creator of the B minor Piano Sonata, but what sort of listeners might these be? Perhaps we ought to discriminate between different kinds of listener, at whom different kinds of music are aimed. The classification of music into 'serious' and 'light' makes exactly this assumption. It is, after all, important to know your audience. But again we are faced with the alternative pictures of the listener as a recipient of sensations – generally in the toes, according to Liszt – and of the listener for whom experience means more than sensation, and for whom experience carries the obligation to engage in what he hears – precisely the obligation which Doernberg accuses Hanslick of failing to discharge. But what is this that is 'more than sensation'? This is something we shall have to find out.

Percy Scholes's approach to the problem of musical experience is rhetorical and abrupt:

> What, after all, *is* romance in music? How *is* it achieved? Why *should* this strangely simple piece of Chopin with its underlying oft-repeated left-hand figures and its plain-sailing right-hand melody ... why should it lull and fascinate us? Can anyone say? Perhaps if they could there would be no romance. Is romance the employment of a sixth sense? Is it the perception of the unknown?[11]

Is there life on Mars? Murky stuff. On the one hand Scholes might be cautioning against attempts to analyse figurative language – including what he calls 'romance' – on logical grounds, for instance that truth conditions will be hard to come by. And the 'sixth sense' which he dangles in front of us could be sought in an account of the operation of metaphor in more general language – some sophisticated faculty which we develop from experience in an important area of language, including aesthetic discourse. But, of course, Scholes may mean no such thing. He may be invoking a particularly acute and ineffable 'aesthetic' sensibility (perhaps rather like the 'aesthetic emotion' of a philosophical aesthetician such as Clive Bell). And to talk of the 'perception of the unknown' certainly has this mystical air. Perhaps, to borrow a religious metaphor, art somehow 'speaks to our condition'. The only proviso would be that our condition was properly sensitised and somehow attuned to the particularly diaphanous wavelength which 'romance' occupied in the aesthetic ether.

That some such external agency operates in the case of musical sounds themselves seems to be assumed by Paul Hindemith's deification of the major triad of the diatonic scale:

> Tones 1–6 of the overtones series . . . outline the extended major triad, which is to the *trained and the naive listener alike* one of the most impressive phenomena of Nature, simple and elemental as rain, snow and wind. Music, as long as it exists, will always take its departure from the major triad and return to it.[12]
>
> (My emphasis.)

Evidently anyone can apply for the position of listener; no previous experience is necessary. But is this really true? Who might a naive listener be? Well, perhaps someone from a culture where the diatonic implications of the overtone series were not thought paramount; say an Indian or Chinese. Hindemith's confidence is unshaken by little local difficulties like these, for

> In the world of tones, the triad corresponds to the force of gravity. It serves as our constant guiding point, our unit of measure, and our goal, even in those sections of compositions which seem to avoid it.[13]

And there follows an elaborate argument to prove his point. Of course if he is thinking of atonal developments within the diatonic tradition, Hindemith must know what he is talking about. But the force of gravity is usually thought to have wider application; for instance gravity is binding upon those who can never reflect on it, like statues, hedgehogs and nasturtiums. So is Hindemith really suggesting that the major triad depends on no conscious relation between the sound and the listener? Is he really saying that the triad does not need to be in a sense 'read' as such? Does it really hold sway over all listeners, even those whose picture of the overtone series makes no reference to the diatonic scale? Are all listeners equally in thrall to this aural despot?

It seems, then, from these extracts, that two alternative pictures of the listener emerge, between which we must arbitrate. The one is of a passive recipient of the sensations that come his way; the other is of someone actively engaging in what he hears. The passive, patient listener simply experiences and utters accordingly, as though his emotions were stimulated and played upon by an external agency, be it the performer, the composer or simply the universal vibrations themselves. According to this picture, any programmatic aspects are simply, as it were, presented to him for his contemplation; his perception is unmediated by judgement, compliant, spontaneous. And if his judgements are idiosyncratic, they are no worse than those of his fellows. This is what the music says to him, and that's that. In the absence of truth conditions, his figurative judgements may be perplexing; or we may simply 'know what he means' by the happy accident that our own moods have been set wobbling at the same frequency. As for his qualifications, these are marginal – the basic building blocks of music, such as the major triad, are part of the common weal, available on demand. Experience is mostly a matter of a collection of sensations, to which he can refer retrospectively as comforting confirmation that his sensibilities are becoming more and more attuned. He can say with pride that he knows what the music means to him on the intensely personal level, and who can gainsay him? And the troublesome technical vocabulary of analysis may serve as a helpful series of pegs on which he can hang his judgements, but they are ultimately dispensable. The poetic and figurative language which he uses is justified by its reality *for him*; and the connections with the technical descriptions of what he hears are at best tenuous, more probably irrelevant. He awaits the music, and it simply speaks to him.

On the other hand, the alternative picture to emerge is one of a participant listener, engaging in and operating upon what he hears – bringing it under judgement. According to this picture, his feelings are secondary to – indeed, arise from – his judgements. And the judgements that he makes are subject to the approval of other listeners. His figurative language represents the end of a process of something like searching the music for aspects which satisfy him. And these will, in principle, be available to others for their inspection. Hence his figurative language can be examined and assessed, and if necessary rejected. His qualifications as a listener, moreover, will draw on the kinds of aural distinctions which are described by the technical vocabulary of criticism. Indeed the *possibility* of technical descriptions will be integral to his figurative accounts of what he hears. His figurative language, divorced from truth conditions, will instead require some other philosophical account of how they can be understood and assented to by others. For him, experience will mean a developing ability to engage in music in a directed way. He participates in what he hears. The music will not of itself speak to him – he must read it.

Each of these pictures has its attractions and each its problems. Superficially the picture of the patient listener is closer to the way we often like to feel about music. Basking in the glow from Gilels's recording of a Busoni/Bach transcription I can easily feel that the music has washed over me, assailed my senses, spoken to my condition. I am limp and helpless before it. Yet this picture fails to say why I am like this, or how I came to be able to feel like that. It fails to discuss the 'condition' to which the music is supposed to speak: the mode of attention under which I listen.

On the other hand, the picture of the participant listener seems better fitted to account for the nature of my attention to music, and for the judgements that ensue from the encounter. Yet it seems to rest on an ambitious promise – the promise of an account of how my figurative responses to music may be underwritten in a publicly significant and available manner, in the absence of any conditions for their truth or falsity. And the provision of such an account seems a daunting task.

I quoted a short part of Neville Cardus's review of the playing of Horowitz as an example of a particularly acute and intriguing image: one that seemed, in isolation, to defy penetration. But I quoted it out of context. And the very fact that, replaced in that context, it takes on meaning, is in itself an important signal that context, direction and judgement are vital here. It signals to us that the picture of the active, searching, interpreting listener is the important one, the one that we should establish and explore. For it is in the context of judgement that the language of feeling and of image have sense and direction, point and purpose. It will be my task to show how we can understand and accept the language of imagery, even in the absence of criteria for its significance.

But first, let us replace Cardus's remark in its context:

> Horowitz makes the most stupendous technical difficulties
> sound like child's play.... It is easier in music to lean on
> 'philosophy' than it is to make music. Horowitz has the genius to
> ravish the piano and yet leave it chaste. Horowitz and the piano
> are one and indivisible.... He distills the essence of a chord.
> Never, not even when he is thrilling our ears by his great bravura
> playing, is he merely a virtuoso. His technique faithfully serves
> the composer's imaginative inventions. He plays Liszt in the
> grand manner, but with a refinement of touch and balance of
> tone which expel vulgarity altogether. The most familiar *Hun-
> garian Rhapsody* of Liszt loses, at the fingers of Horowitz, all
> hackneyed assocations, all phoney swagger. He removes the
> dandruff.[14]

I think that only one who participated in what he heard could have
said that.

Notes

1. John Foulds, *Music Today* (Ivor Nicholson & Watson, 1934), p. 179.
2. Ferruccio Busoni, 'A New Esthetic of Music' (in *Three Classics in the Aesthetics of Music*, Dover Publications, 1962), p. 82.
3. Robert Layton, *Sibelius* (J. M. Dent, 1965), p. 79.
4. Busoni, *New Esthetic*.
5. Alan Walker, *Franz Liszt – The Virtuoso Years* (Faber & Faber, 1983), p. 291.
6. Donald Francis Tovey, *Essays in Musical Analysis*, Vol. V, (Oxford University Press, 1937), p. 40.
7. Wilfrid Mellers, *Bach and the Dance of God* (Faber & Faber, 1980), pp. 55–6.
8. Neville Cardus, Notes to Columbia recording of Horowitz (MQ 499, 1962), p. 11.
9. Erwin Doernberg, *The Life and Symphonies of Anton Bruckner* (Barrie & Rockliffe, 1960), p. 67.
10. (Quoted in) Arthur Hedley, *Chopin* (J. M. Dent, 1947), p. 149.
11. Percy A. Scholes, *The Listener's History of Music* (Oxford University Press, 1923), p. 24.
12. Paul Hindemith, *The Craft of Musical Composition* (Associated Music Publishers, 1937), p. 22.
13. Ibid.
14. Cardus, Notes.

2

Emotion

Our interest in music arises from its intimate relation to the all-important life of feeling, whatever that relation may be. . . .[1]

This is as good an example as any of the circumscription that is generally made of the problem of musical expression. That is, it is generally assumed that if anything needs explaining, it is the connection between music (the food of love) and the emotions it expresses on the one hand, and the way we perceive and understand that expression on the other.

Musicians are valued according to how much 'soul' they have, how much they 'give' of themselves in performance. The philistine is one who 'feels' nothing, who is 'unmoved' by art. The great composer is he who has suffered much; the sympathetic listener he whose capacious bosom discerns and responds to the emotions the composer has brought forth.

It will not be my concern to try and dispute any connection at all between music and emotion. What I want to find out is how much is explained by the connections which exist; how much it helps us to suppose that music is primarily the expression of emotion. It is only because this supposition is so widespread that I believe it to be necessary to bring it under sceptical scrutiny. In particular, it is because the preoccupation with emotion has led aestheticians to identify emotion with insight, that a worthwhile philosophical job is to be done in demolishing this most cherished of creeds.

The ubiquity of the fascination with emotion can be brought out by a genuinely cursory glance at what musicians, listeners and philosophers have to say on the subject. For instance, to continue the paragraph from Langer with which I opened:

The function of music is not stimulation of feeling, but expression of it; and furthermore, not the symptomatic expression of feelings that beset the composer but a symbolic expression of the forms of sentience as he understands them. It bespeaks his

15

imagination of feelings rather than his own emotional state, and expresses what he knows about the so-called 'inner life'.[2]

Notice that while this is quite a sophisticated story, distinguishing between what a composer expresses and what he concurrently feels, the assumption is plain that the proper business of music is with feelings. Richard Wagner offers us a less fastidious account, linking the inner disturbances with the end product:

> When a musician feels prompted to sketch the smallest composition, he owes it simply to the stimulus of a feeling which usurps his whole being at the hour of conception. This mood may be brought about by an outward experience or have risen from a secret inner spring; whether it shows itself as melancholy, joy, desire, contentment, love or hatred, in the musician it will always take a musical shape, and voice itself in tones or ever it is cast in notes. But grand, passionate and lasting emotions, dominating all our feelings and ideas for months and often half a year, these drive the musician to those vaster, more intense conceptions to which we owe, among others, the origin of a 'Sinfonia eroica'. These greater moods, as deep suffering of soul or potent exaltation, may date from outer causes, for we all are men and our fate is ruled by outward circumstances; but when they force the musician to production these greater moods have already turned to music in him, so that at the moment of creative inspiration it is no longer the outer event that governs the composer, but the musical sensation it has begotten in him.[3]

Franz Liszt was inclined to agree, and regarded the performer as standing to his programme in more or less exactly the same relation as does the composer to his offspring:

> For the virtuoso, musical works are in fact nothing but tragic and moving materialisations of his emotions; he is called upon to make them speak, weep, sing and sigh, to re-create them in accordance with his own consciousness. In this way, he like the composer, is a creator, for he must have within himself those passions which he wishes so intensely to bring to life.[4]

Now one hesitates to take issue with great men, so as a matter of prudence I shall do so only obliquely. For we are not told why the emotions of the composer take the form they do, or why they are articulated in this medium and form rather than that, or, indeed, why they are articulated at all, in distinction from the passions of thousands of ordinary men. We are told nothing of the connection between the form of the idea and the nature of the germinal emotion.

And it is further worth noting that, whatever Wagner may be claiming, his assertions could entail only that emotions were, in his experience, a sufficient condition for the production of some music or other: and not a necessary one. For Wagner, music may have been an inevitable accompaniment to emotion, but he certainly does not tell us that emotion is the inevitable source of music. (It is interesting to notice that when Byron said, 'All convulsion ends with me in rhyme' he did not specify convulsion as the necessary precondition of his work.[5] He did not say, 'All rhyme begins with me in convulsion'.)

So even accepting Wagner's claims would not bind us to the idea that all music has even an empirical connection with emotion. Nor should it lead us to suppose that any questions about the mechanism of composition had been answered: they have not, but they have been deflected.

Deryck Cooke, in his *The Language of Music*, offered an elaborate guide to the notational connections between musical phrase-types, and alleged items of emotional experience. Early on in his book, he gives us a kind of manifesto indicating what is involved in competent listening:

> Music is, properly speaking, a language of the emotions, akin to speech. The appeal of this music is directly to the emotions, and to be fully appreciated, should be responded to in this way. The widespread view of music as 'purely music' limits the listener's understanding of the great masterpieces to their purely aural beauty – i.e., to their surface attraction – and to their purely technical construction. This latter is no more (and no less) than the magnificent craftsmanship whereby composers express their emotions coherently, and is ultimately inexplicable to almost anyone but a potential composer. Music is, in fact, 'extra-musical' in the sense that poetry is 'extra-verbal' since notes, like words, have emotional connotations; it is, let me repeat, the supreme expression of universal emotions, in an entirely personal way, by the great composers.[6]

I am tempted to remark here that, in my opinion, this is just about as mistaken an account of music as it is possible to produce. The aural 'surface' of the music is claimed to be merely vehicular with respect to the musical inspiration; but a moment's thought shows these to be utterly indistinguishable: it is in the notes themselves, and nowhere else, that we discern the ideas of a given work – or better, the ideas are constituted by the notes and by nothing else. The claim that music is 'extra-musical' defies analysis. And the idea that the music is simply the 'craftsmanship' employed by the composers to express the emotions which presumably are the 'real' import of what they have to say, on Cooke's account, robs the music of any but an accidental or causal connection with the idea to be articulated. It is difficult to see how Cooke could evade the charge that on his view, the musical idea might as easily have been manifested in sculpture. And this would be to descend into idealism of the worst kind.

But the crucial complaint (and that most pertinent to my present enquiry) concerns Cooke's claim that 'The appeal of this music is directly to the emotions, and to be fully appreciated, should be responded to in this way'. For a start, it seems strange to exhort anyone to make an emotional response; to lay it down as a condition to be fulfilled, as it were mechanically, or as part of a method. Emotions are not like that. Anyway, we want to ask Cooke, is that *all*? What is the basis for our response? What is it that puts us in a position to be moved? (Or even to want to be moved?) If Cooke replied that he had given us, in the course of his book, the gazetteer of emotion particulars which we could apply, then we should certainly ask where the link lay between merely recognising the correct application of a code, and coming to hear emotion in the notes themselves.

It is not simply that there is an inherent implausibility about a notation of feelings; it is further that this could not be an explanation of being moved. Rather it sounds like a procedure for interpretation. Again, Cooke's thesis gives us no inkling of what criticism could amount to. For if it seeks to discern the adequacy of the composer's technique to his motivic ideas, which on Cooke's thesis appear fundamentally to be emotions, that adequacy could be judged only by reference to some independent scale of reading which did not rely on the relation between the phrase particulars of Cooke's catalogue and the items of emotion experience. But

Cooke seems to hold that the phrase particulars are the basic ingredients of judgement.

Indeed, it is this assumption of feelings into judgements that troubles me most. I do not want to deny the links between music and emotions; but I do want to deny that emotions constitute some kind of pre-cognitive understanding, and I want to deny that they embody the explanation of what it is to understand music. But it is precisely this that Cooke seems to affirm.

What then of the aesthetic attitude – that attitude characteristic of the contemplation of music as 'art'? If emotion is to explain anything here, it must account for our seeking a particular kind of articulation, namely the expressive, and for why we approach art in a way characteristically different from the way we approach familiar, everyday emotional disturbances. One writer who attempts this is Antony Hopkins, in a pithy passage from his book *Talking about Sonatas*:

> A third rate composer can simulate grief perfectly well, but in the long run, it is only the grief of a seven-year-old. Beethoven's pain was the pain of an adult, an adult moreover who had suffered so much that he was able to transcend the personal and become universal. It is the Christian belief that Christ carried the burden of our sins. I do not consider it blasphemous to say that Bach, Mozart and Beethoven carried the burden of our sorrows.[7]

This astonishing claim is clearly heading towards a cathartic explanation of the attitude in which we approach music. We shun or dismiss the lesser because it does not sublimate the kind of grief that the greater does. Admittedly, Hopkins says 'simulate', not 'sublimate', and thus he owes us an account of how this simulation is to take place. But more importantly, it is far from certain that we approach music in anything like this manner. No doubt we *can* approach it like this; but only if we are first in a position to understand, to get to grips with the music as expressive. That is, it surely will not do to suppose that the reading of the mechanical processes of the relationships between the notes is merely a stimulant to unblock our psychic ducts. If there are circumstances in which music can do that unblocking, we want to be told more about the circumstances themselves. But they are not, it seems clear, characteristic of our approach to music. We do not refrain

from confronting music until we are in a suitably overwrought
state; rather we are best able to contemplate the musical argument
from a position of detachment, an attitude of placidity. And should
we find ourselves in need of a cathartic experience, it is not at all
clear that we standardly seek an encounter with art.

The emotional approach to the aesthetic attitude has its final
fling in the identification of that attitude with a peculiar and quite
idiosyncratic emotion, namely, the 'aesthetic' emotion, whose
principal advocates have been, I suppose, Clive Bell and Roger Fry.
The catch-all nature of this 'emotion' comes out in this passage
from Fry's *Vision and Design*: 'In proportion as art becomes purer
the number of people to whom it appeals gets less. . . . It appeals
only to the aesthetic sensibility, and that in most men is comparatively weak.'[8] And evidently in the remainder of men it is totally
self-authenticating.

Lastly among these exploratory remarks, I turn to philosophers
engaged in the search for an account of the grammar, as it were, of
our understanding of music, or of art more generally. To return to
the estimable Susanne Langer:

> The tonal structures we call music bear a close logical similarity
> to the forms of human feeling – forms of growth and of
> attenuation, flowing and stowing, conflict and resolution, speed,
> arrest, terrific excitement, calm or subtle activation, and dreamy
> lapses – not joy or sorrow perhaps but the poignancy of either
> and both – the greatness and brevity and eternal passing of
> everything vitally felt. Such is the pattern, or logical form, of
> sentience and the pattern of music is that same form worked out
> in pure, measured sound and silence. Music is a tonal analogue
> of emotive life.[9]

Now here is a philosopher's answer to the question we raised in
connection with that 'simulation' of which Hopkins spoke. Langer's account of music in *Philosophy in a New Key* is precisely that it
supplies, via a scheme of 'unconsummated symbols', a logical
analogue of the form of human emotion. Yet this seems to afford
the emotions themselves some kind of precognitive status, unargu-
ably given (and grimly swallowed). It withdraws emotions from
the cognitive contexts in which alone they can occur. It seems to
cut out any questions as to how we can depict the logical form of
emotions *in order to judge* the suitability of the musical analogue. By

virtue of what, we want to know, do we understand the similarity of logical form? Whatever the answer is, it cannot consist in a further appeal to our emotions. But, if it consists in something else – as it surely must – then *that something* is the epistemological basis of our appraisal of music, and not our emotion.

Langer is not alone in supposing a central epistemological problem to lie in the account of the expression of emotion. Perhaps the best among the recent writers on aesthetics, Richard Wollheim, makes the same assumption explicit in his discussion of expression in *Art and Its Objects*:

> When we turn from the problem of representational properties to that of expressive properties and how they bear on the identification of works of art with physical objects, the situation somewhat changes. For the problem seems to be not, How can a work of art qua physical object express this or that emotion? but, How can a work of art qua physical object express emotion?[10]

and

> It is not at all clear that, in the cases where we attribute emotions to objects in the ways that I have tried to describe, we have any other way of talking about the objects themselves.[11]

Wollheim could hardly be more insistent on the centrality of the emotion question, as he continues, identifying the problem of expression as the problem of the expression of emotion, thus: 'To put *the same point* in non-linguistic terms, it is not always the case that the things that we see as expressive, we can or could see in any other way'.[12]   (My emphasis.)

My complaint about the foregoing could be summed up like this: no doubt there is an important connection between the expressive powers of music and human emotion, but in what sense can this area furnish us with an explanation of our understanding of music? The enquiry, How does music move us? is primarily a psychological, not a philosophical nor even, I contend, a musical enquiry. And to the extent that philosophers have concentrated on seeking to explain this connection, I believe they have wasted their energy: this question is an external one. What we do need to know is, How comes about the understanding which enables us to be moved – or not to be moved – as the case may be? And this enquiry cannot be answered by appealing to our emotions, as I intend to show in more detail.

In fact it is at precisely this point that the question of emotion appears in a legitimate role. For among the many sorts of predicates that are ascribed to pieces of music and to performances, emotion terms are fairly prominent. So it is clear that an account of how mental predicates (and of course others whose application to music is not their primary one) can in fact be applied to music would be a very valuable one. I hope to outline such an account in the remaining chapters, and also to suggest where others have begun such an account.

If we examine some traditional attempts to account for the appearance of these emotion predicates, we find that precisely those mistaken assumptions (about the explanatory role of emotion) of which I have complained, seem to dominate the approach taken. Interestingly, the two philosophers I have mentioned – Langer and Wollheim – see the inadequacies of the traditional attempts at explanation, without either of them overcoming the fascination for regarding emotion as in some sense explanatory.

Thus, traditional accounts of the application of emotion terms to pieces of music have lodged them in the direct expression of the composer's feelings, sympathetically or empathetically received by a passive listener. This is a crude, but not unfair summary. Many writers have pointed out the obvious empirical inadequacy of the 'direct expression' thesis: namely that there are simply too many instances of happy composers writing sad tunes (and vice versa) for there to be any reasonable correlation here. Others have foreseen logical and epistemological difficulties. Carnap has pointed out that art as sheer self-expression is not to be distinguished from inarticulate cries, a view that would bracket the fourteenth Goldberg variation with the yelp of a Cairn terrier. Carnap seems to have concluded that these were therefore scarcely to be distinguished epistemologically. On the other hand, Susanne Langer correctly inferred that this simply means that sheer self-expression requires no artistic form, and as such simply cannot account for the production of art.

The laws of emotional catharsis are natural laws, not artistic ... even the expressiveness of oaths rests not on the fact that such words were invented for psycho-cathartic purposes, but that they are taboo, and the breaking of a taboo gives emotional release. Breaking a vase would do better still.[13]

Or as Huw Morris-Jones has put it, in 'The Language of Feelings':

> What quirk of human psychology induces a man who is sexually aroused to write a love lyric rather than to find relief in a less indirect form of satisfaction? And, more perplexing still, why should anyone else, apart from psychiatrists or those fond of pseudo-psychological speculations, be interested in the product of these expressive functions? It seems clear that those who write like this have little experience of art and no understanding of it.[14]

In fact, it is precisely this relocation of the central interest in what must, after all, be simple biographical data, that is the fatal flaw in the direct expression theory. Wollheim himself makes the point as well as anyone:

> What is probably the more fundamental objection to this view is ... that the work's expressiveness now becomes a purely external feature of it. It is no longer something that we can or might observe, it is something that we infer from what we might observe: it has been detached from the object as it manifests itself to us, and placed in its history, so that it now belongs more to the biography of the artist than to criticism of the work.[15]

A further view is centred on the effect which the work produces in the listener – a work is expressive of emotion because it is productive of emotion. Again this is first of all open to simply empirical objections. The idea that the listener would need vicariously to indulge in sundry idealised poles of grief, melancholy or despair would lead us to doubt whether anyone ever went to a concert or played a record voluntarily. I believe it is Hegel who says that art is 'essentially cheerful'. This seems a rather flippant way of putting the matter, but certainly nearer the mark than the postulation of various unsolicited bouts of misery, anguish and other associated turmoils. Listening to music is, on the whole, rather enjoyable. (It might be objected that one could want to experience the uplifting effect of music of a more vigorous and triumphal character. But, still at the empirical level, this would fail to explain why concerts of 'tragic' music are at least as well subscribed as those of a more jolly content.)

In a similar vein, we may complain of Franz Liszt's notion that the virtuoso produces 'materialisations of his emotions' in performance, that if this were really the case a performer would undergo such paroxysmal changes of disposition and nervous trauma during the course of a typical programme of mid-nineteenth-century music as to develop acute schizophrenia. But the challenge for the performer is surely rather to communicate from that position of detachment in which alone he can control the unfolding of the musical tapestry.

Of course it is plain that these empirical objections must immediately make room for the more fundamental, logical objection offered against the 'direct expression' account. For even if there were some sort of thrill for the listener in playing at being temporarily (and of course remediably) lovelorn, bereaved or victorious or what-have-you, this is not a primarily aesthetic response; for it reduces the music to a somatic or causal role, and the listener to a sort of aural junkie. Of course it would be foolish of me to deny that this takes place; what I deny is that this is what constitutes understanding – rather I shall argue that this kind of response depends on a prior understanding of the work.

Edouard Hanslick, writing in a pre-psychedelic age, makes effectively the same point in connection with different 'ersatz' responses:

> Music may, undoubtedly, awaken feelings of great joy, or intense sorrow, but might not the same or a still greater effect be produced by the news that we have won first prize in a lottery, or by the dangerous illness of a friend? So long as we refuse to include lottery tickets amongst the symphonies, or medical bulletins amongst the overtures, we must refrain from treating the emotions as an aesthetic monopoly of music in general, or of a certain piece of music in particular.[16]

Richard Wollheim puts the point in philosophical language:

> The main objection to this view ... is that it removes what we ordinarily think of as (one of the) essential characteristics of the work of art from among its manifest properties, locating it this time not in its past but in its hidden or dispositional endowment.[17]

Curiously, after this clear exegesis, Wollheim makes two inter-dependent attempts to rescue just this combined account of expression, that is, the account tying the expressive power of the art-object to what its producer or its observers themselves feel. I shall maintain my attack on this traditional view, therefore, by demonstrating the failure of Wollheim's rescue attempts.

Firstly, Wollheim tries to redeem the claims about what composers and listeners feel, by modification. Underpinning this attempt is a legitimate concern that we should never take emotion predicates seriously in connection with works of art if they had no general connections whatsoever with people's states of mind. This is a just and an important insistence. But we should note at the outset that it need by no means lead to actual individual connections with what given people feel on specifiable occasions. Wollheim half-acknowledges this in his first rescue attempt. In section 16 of *Art and its Objects*, Wollheim posits the substitution, for claims about what given composers and listeners feel, of claims about what hypothetical composers and listeners might have felt in circumstances leading to the production of, or accompanying the listening to, a given work. In such and such a frame of mind, this (x) is the sort of art-object I would tend to produce; and, listening to (looking at) this art-object would tend, in general, to produce in me such and such a frame of mind (x).

Now Wollheim might be doing one of two things here. He might be trying to give general conditions of intelligibility for a way of talking (that of using emotion terms in connection with art-objects) such that the connections do not depend on any empirical connec-tions between given art-objects and individuals' actual states of mind. (We have already noted the fatal empirical objections to claiming such links.) This would form the background to an account of the appropriateness of that way of talking which could, in principle, deal with the objections concerning the extrinsic nature of actual feelings. But of course in this case Wollheim would need to proceed to give us such an account.

Alternatively, Wollheim might be attempting to cover those cases where, as a matter of fact, an emotional experience is not involved, by some kind of extension from those cases where, as a matter of fact, one is. If this is the case, then of course he simply takes us back – via a circuitous route – to our original objection that the emotional response had a merely causal relation with the art-object.

Which of these alternatives does Wollheim pursue? In sections 17 and 18, he attempts to narrow the gap between the categorical and the hypothetical claims about what the composer/listener actually feels. To do this, he introduces the notion of feelings to which one stands in a relation other than the 'primary' one of conscious experience. It is worth quoting the relevant passage in full:

> For as long as we confine ourselves to conscious feelings or feelings which we experience primarily, there is obviously a substantial gap between the supposition that something or other is what we would have felt if we had made a certain object, and the assertion that this is what the person who made it felt: and, again, between the supposition that we would feel in such and such a way before a certain object in other circumstances, and the assertion that this is what we really feel before it. But enlarge the conception of human feelings, extend it so as to take in the whole range of psychic states, and the situation considerably changes. There is still, of course, a gap, but the gap has so shrunk that it is sometimes thought to be no wider than can be crossed by the leap from evidence to conclusion. In other words, a speculation about what I would have felt in someone else's situation or in other circumstances can, in favoured conditions, be warrant enough for an assertion about what that person really feels, or about our own hidden emotions.[18]

It seems clear, then, that it is the second alternative – that of covering the cases where, empirically, feelings are not involved, by extension from the cases where they are – which Wollheim wishes to pursue. For what the story about the 'enlarged conception of human feelings' achieves is to pull the hypothetical cases back towards the categorical; to bolster the categorical claims which seem not to be true by the supposition that they really are true, but in some less than 'primary' sense. Apart from the inherent implausibility of this view, the account runs immediately into the original objection: what relation can the feelings, which some people may actually undergo, have with the art-object other than a merely causal one? For if we simply substitute, for the claim that a work of art makes me feel x, the claim that it would ordinarily tend to make me feel x (by extension from the cases where I subconsciously feel x, remember what feeling x is like, or identify myself with other people who do in fact feel x in these circumstances) we have still done nothing to tie the feeling logically to the understanding of this art-object.

Wollheim's second rescue attempt is more involved: I will show that it is simply open to a more involved rebuttal. In this case, Wollheim claims that the concept of expression as applied to art is basically an 'intersection' of two 'constituent notions of expression'. In section 18 he reveals these constituent notions which turn out to be none other than, first,

> expressive in the sense in which a gesture or a cry would be expressive: this is to say, we conceive of it coming so immediately and directly out of some emotional or mental state that it bears unmistakable marks of that state upon it.

And, second,

> an object (as) expressive of a certain condition because, when we are in that condition, it seems to us to match, or correspond with, what we experience inwardly: and perhaps when the condition passes, the object is also good for reminding us of it in some special poignant way, or for reviving it for us.[19]

The first of these constituents then is the self-expression of which we have already disposed; the second is as honest an account as we could wish of the straightforward abuse of an art-object for somatic purposes. Again this is instantly open to the original and by now well-rehearsed objection.

However, Wollheim makes the argument more sophisticated by considering the ways in which these constituents 'interact'. The crucial feature, he says, is: 'the notion of appropriateness, or fittingness, conceived as a relation holding between expression and expressed'.[20] And Wollheim links the obvious aspects of fittingness in connection with correspondences, with direct self-expression in this way:

> In reality, at any level above the most primitive, natural expression will always be coloured or influenced by some sense of what is appropriate: there will be a feedback from judgement, however inchoate or unconscious this may be, to gesture or exclamation.[21]

The trouble is, it is no longer clear just how 'direct' the direct self-expression is supposed to be. And this is precisely what we should expect in an artistic articulation. We would expect it to be informed by judgement, and to be properly understood only as such. But now, of course, we seem no longer to be talking about 'feelings'. For Wollheim's insistence on the appropriate, on the 'feedback from judgement', is the triumph of his sounder instincts over his visible enterprise. He wants to root the expressive quality of art in direct expression; and to make the account plausible, he has to beef up the notion of direct expression to the sort of cognitive, informed, articulate level which simply does not feature in the original notion. He wants to show us how a feeling can be informed and discursive, so he paints for us a system of judgement – but the feeling has disappeared.

I said earlier that had Wollheim been attempting to give us an account of the appropriateness of emotion terms as applied to art, we should have been interested. His talk about the 'feedback from judgement' suggests that this is what he would like to have done. In fact, however, he has demonstrated – by the failure of his rescue attempt – just why no understanding of expression can ever be based on feelings: for feelings are not themselves cognitive or discursive, whereas judgements are. And it is in this context of judgements that an understanding is formed; it is within an understanding that a feeling can arise. The special poignancy of causal association is possible only when a reading has been made of the art-object, such that an association is produced. To recall my earlier complaint, no doubt there is an important connection between emotion and the expressive power of music, but this cannot be explained by appealing to our resultant feelings – only by setting out the conditions of judgement and understanding within which alone can we be moved. Any art-object – indeed, any phenomenon whatever – can move us, according to wider circumstances which we may require to be spelled out. Whether, and why, we are moved will depend on the reading we make. The reading may be explained by an appeal to judgement, and not to feelings.

The late Artur Schnabel was known for his powers of pianism and interpretation, rather than for his philosophical insight. But the latter is very much in evidence in this story, related by André Previn, of Schnabel's refusals to commit any performance to a recording:

Schnabel was one of the last pianists to record. All his colleagues had been recording, but he refused. He said 'I have a terrible fear of making a record of a Beethoven sonata and somewhere, some day, someone is going to listen to it while eating a liverwurst sandwich'.[22]

It is perhaps easy to see why the emotion account, once it is current, tends to suppress our appreciation of the importance of the reading. For emotions, though rooted in judgement, have an aura of passivity about them. The emotion account of music emphasises a passive and patient listener, manipulated and dandled by the composer and interpreter. Later I shall argue how there is something of this in the reading processes themselves – how their very familiarity obscures their participatory nature. This central obscuring of the activity of listening is perhaps my main motivation in wanting to tackle the emotion account of music.

How has the account, particularly in the traditional forms we have examined, attained such currency (even ubiquity)? I think we could give both historical and philosophical reasons. We could look for historical reasons in the shifting of the musical enterprise at given moments in musical development towards a programmatic approach – when emotions, perhaps the most easily grasped among many sorts of programme material, became prominent. This enterprise has its founding fathers, its disciples, its prophets and its faithful, as Bujic has pointed out.[23] But equally it has its historical and cultural limits; and very plainly the greater part of musical history is not concerned with this programmatic approach; the greater part of music does not wear its heart on its sleeve, but has enterprises more readily described by reference to other kinds of human endeavours and aspirations – architecture for instance. Of course, it remains for us to account for the appropriateness of the emotion predicates in the cases where they are important, and I have declared my intention to get to grips with this as one task among many similar and related tasks.

Another explanation of the currency of the emotion account could employ philosophical reasons. In particular, I have in mind the distinction between the 'presentational' and the 'affective' usages of emotion terms. This distinction is already latent in the second of Wollheim's attempts, above, to redeem the emotion account. When he talks about self-expression, he links this to actual felt emotional states. We may term these actual disturbances

in people 'affective' emotion. When Wollheim talks about the
correspondence between objects (as expressive of a certain condition) and the condition itself, he brings to bear both affective and
the 'presentational' senses of emotion. The object may be said to
'present' emotions to us, corresponding, Wollheim claims, to the
conditions which affect us. The emotions which are often said to be
'in' objects, or stories, or musical passages, then, we can term
'presentational' emotions – emotions which are presented, or
depicted. Clearly one can contemplate the depiction of joy or
suffering without oneself being affected. It all depends on the
wider circumstances involved. We can take presentational emotions seriously enough, for instance in a reconstruction of evidence
in a crime of passion, without ourselves being affected. Equally as I
have shown, one can be moved, even deeply moved, by any
phenomenon whatever, provided that wider circumstances include the possibility of the appropriate reading. The sight of a road
sign indicating that one is within reach of home may occasion all
kinds of affects in us, but no emotion is 'presented' to us in this
sort of case. Of course, there is nothing new in any of this: the
distinction between hearing the sadness in a tune, and being
oneself sad, has been elaborated on at length and by many writers.
I am less sure, however, that the distinction has been taken
seriously enough, even by those very writers who have been at
pains to stress it. At any rate, let us for the present notice that it is
very easy indeed to fall foul of the distinction; to move from the
legitimate recognition of 'presentational' emotion to the spurious
supposition that affective emotion must somehow be involved in
the proper response. This move becomes easier still when we
remember that the terms 'presentational' and 'affective' will not
ordinarily figure in the vocabulary of those making the move; and
here I include musicians, musicologists, critics, performers, composers and philosophers, who appear to reserve their grammatical
fastidiousness for the study, the record player being in the lounge.
Thus, 'This is a sad tune' is almost universally elided into 'This
tune makes me sad', although the elision will not appear until
people are asked to say what understanding musical expression
consists in. Then they will tell us the sort of thing that Deryck
Cooke has told us: 'The appeal of music is directly to the emotions,
and to be fully appreciated, should be responded to in this way.'
(see p. 17, above).

I have hinted of an account of the application of emotion terms to music; I shall now pave the way for such an account by considering further the operation of 'presentational' terms, and by further examining the mysterious 'aesthetic' emotion that has sometimes been offered as the true and proper attitude in the approach to art. These two enquiries will occupy us for the rest of this chapter.

The problem of the presentation of emotion in an art-object (let us say, a piece of music) is the problem of explaining how we understand the appropriateness of characterisations of the music which involve emotion terms. This is, I think, clear from the distinction we have been at pains to make between the emotion that we hear and the emotion that we feel. What is it, therefore, to hear a tune as sad, as melancholy, as triumphal, as earnest, and so on?

It seems to me that this is just one facet of a more general problem: What is it to hear a tune *as* anything at all? What is it to hear a piece of music as being under a given description? Emotion terms are one kind of imagery among many other kinds; so the problem of explaining this kind of image is part of the problem of explaining imagery in general. It has to be said that the traditional approach to the question of emotion terms has not regarded them as part of such a wider problem. Rather there has been a fascination about the sense in which emotion can inhere or feature in a melody, which has driven writers to explain just this one kind of aspect by special senses of being 'in' a tune; or by special senses of the emotion term involved; or even, in the case of Langer, by a special kind of symbolic relation between the melody and the emotion it is said to 'present'.

For instance, Ronald Hepburn thinks the burden of explanation lies in an account of what 'in' means, in the idea of the presentation of emotion 'in' music: 'I think the stronger prima facie case can be made out for the account which claims that emotional qualities can be described with perfect propriety as being IN works of art'[24] although 'to claim that the emotional quality can be in the work of art is not of course to say that "in" is used in precisely the same sense as when an emotion is said to be "in" you or me. People experience emotions: works of art do not.'[25] Nevertheless,

Within the classical idiom we feel that in most contexts a dominant seventh, and more so a thirteenth, 'want' to move to the tonic chord. The music wants, strives to reach its own resolution: the wanting is not mine who hear the chord but the music's. This is one of ITS vicissitudes. If the music modulates into a bright key, the brightness is not my brightness but the music's. The music has its own phenomenal career . . .[26]

in as much as 'A piece of music may be in despair, but I who listen enjoyably need by no means be in despair. Almost cautiously, I can relish and savour the anguish of the music: compounding its despair with my delight.'[27]

Well, all good vindictive stuff. The problem here is that Hepburn is not so much explaining imagery as using it – as he later seems to acknowledge. Talk of the music's own 'phenomenal career' cannot explain 'its' sadness or 'its' anything else unless the career is itself explained. Hepburn's instincts are to keep away from identifying what goes on in the music with what goes on in him, but this admirable caution does not stop him from supposing that the music's independent career is still rather like his own – dispositionally different at the moment perhaps, but with a similar agenda. And in this context, disclaimers about the special senses of 'in', as in 'in' the music, do not seem very reassuring. In fact, the burden of the later part of his article is concerned with an account of what our emotions are really like, and with an attempt to transfer this to our judgements about music. And so Hepburn, having hived off the presentational usage of emotion terms from the affective, simply recombines them in some rather mysterious, 'nameless' aesthetic emotions. To this we shall return.

In fact, what may have tempted Hepburn down this road is the criterion that there be an internal relation between the emotion in a description of a piece of music, and the music itself, i.e. that the emotion should characterise the music, not the response. But he took the criterion too literally. For it is simply the internal relation that exists between any characterisation of an object or event, and the object or event itself; namely, that in saying that either the Pennine Way or the Schubert C major Symphony is 'long' you are saying more than that it simply seems long to you. Hepburn quotes O.K. Bouwsma's inimitable way of putting the matter: 'the sadness is to the music rather like the redness to the apple than it is like the burp to the cider'.[28]

It should be immediately plain to us that it is in precisely the case of emotion imagery that we need to be reminded of this internal relation. When we call a melody 'spacious', or a variation 'monolithic', there is little temptation to suppose that this refers to some effect produced in us. ('It makes me feel, well, really monolithic.')

There is another problem with the story that emotions 'inhere' in music in some special sense of 'in'. For unless we are properly acquainted with the way in which emotions are 'in' the music, there no longer seems to be much point in saying that they are there at all. That is, if we are overly cautious about ascribing sadness to a tune, perhaps we cannot expect the ascription to be taken at all seriously. This applies equally, of course, when we are ascribing merely a special sense of the emotion, so that a tune is no longer sad, but merely 'sad'. For in relocating our quotation marks we relocate our hesitancy. Unless calling a tune sad is to convey exactly what we should want to convey in calling a story or an expression or a state of affairs sad, at least half the point seems to be lost.

Langer meets this challenge head-on. She takes it that the emotions which are presented to us in music are, after all, not familiar ones from mundane experience, but special and idiosyncratic ones, simply not specifiable in non-musical terms; the passionate language wielded by musicians and listeners alike constitutes at best an approximation to the sort of thing we should like to have said had a suitable vocabulary been available to us.

Clearly, she owes us an explanation of the inherence of these 'ineffable' presentational emotions in the music, which she requites by an involved and, frankly, astonishing story about musical symbolism. It is worth noticing at once that she is insistent that it is emotional aspects which are central to music, and indeed she displays no interest in any other kind of characterisation.

Now recalling Deryck Cooke, we notice that any story about musical symbolism is to be disregarded if it reduces listening to a kind of map-reading exercise, or to the completion of a sort of crossword puzzle. Music is not a set of signs referring to agreed items of experience. On the other hand, it is difficult to see what a symbol is, if it is not conventionally and conceptually linked to a constant referent.

Langer is deliberately reticent about the identity and nature of any feeling expressed in the art-object. This is inevitable, given that she holds that the identity of that feeling is uniquely tied to the art-object itself, and cannot be independently characterised. She does give us some very general talk about the 'forms of human feeling', as we have already observed, in 'the forms of growth and of attenuation, flowing and stowing, conflict and resolution . . . *not* joy or sorrow perhaps, but the poignancy of either and both'.[29] (My emphasis.) And she also refers to the inconstant, ambiguous and fleeting nature of feelings which are either associated with or felt to be expressed in an art-object, even in one performance or interpretation of that work. 'The assignment of meanings is a shifting, kaleidoscopic play, probably below the threshold of consciousness, certainly outside the pale of discursive thinking.'[30] In fact, the ineffability of those emotions she seeks to consider seems to arise in part from a desire to accommodate conflicting critical readings of one and the same art-object.

However, it is difficult to see what is added to an understanding of music by the claim that the music expresses feelings which cannot be characterised or even identified independently of the work itself. And the more general analogy between the kind of dynamic involved in music (tension and relaxation) and in emotion, seems trivial and unilluminating.

Thus it is clear that one feature of Langer's avowed enterprise in considering the presentation of emotion in music, is to remove certain rather difficult questions about the adequacy of the musical image, the appropriateness of a judgement involving emotion terms, and the grammatical absorption of such judgements into our general schemes of discourse. Langer seems more or less to rule out such questions.

Clive Bell's view of aesthetic emotion was that it was unrelated to everyday experience, and that ordinary emotions were estranged from and indeed irrelevant to it. Now Langer is refining this view, modifying it to allow (even to insist) on important connections between emotion in life and in art, but confining questions about the nature or identity of such connections to the most general – and trivial – level. The evasion of the need to specify what sort of emotion a work expresses, remains.

What sort of a symbol is it, then, that expresses or refers to or signifies something that cannot be distinguished independently of the symbol itself?

Artistic form is congruent with the dynamic forms of our sensuous, mental and emotional life; works of art are projections of our 'felt' life . . . the vital processes of sense and emotion that a good work of art expresses seem to the beholder to be directly contained in it, not symbolised but really presented. The congruence is so striking that symbol and meaning appear as one reality.[31]

Well, this much seems to be sheer mysticism. In *Philosophy in a New Key* she told us that music does not symbolise 'real feeling' but rather 'produces some peculiar effects we mistake for them'.[32]

I think we must see that as an account of symbolism this is so cautious as to amount practically to a withdrawal. Langer toys with the idea of music as a symbolism in the attitude of a fixation, but reluctantly undermines its credibility almost as a matter of instinct. She refers, for instance, to an 'implicit' symbolism, the 'myth of our inner life'. And, less evasively, 'Music has all the earmarks of a true symbolism except one: the existence of an assigned connotation . . . its import is never fixed'.[33]

This is an extremely curious kind of symbol indeed, although the attempt to produce it is consistent with her aversion to independently identifiable feelings, publicly assessible or characterisable, in the music. It appears that we can identify the musical symbols, but not what they signify; we can identify the references but not the referents. But a moment's thought shows us that this is simply to say that the distinction between reference and referent, between symbol and signified, collapses. Of course, this is not in any sense a surprise. What is curious is that Langer should persist in hankering after a symbolism at all in the face of such difficulties.

The lack of an 'assigned connotation' is not just any old 'earmark' of a true symbolism. On the contrary it seems more like a necessary, than a sufficient, condition – a *sine qua non*. Indeed, in the essay on symbolism in *Problems of Art*, Langer effectively concedes this.

A work of art is an expressive form somewhat like a symbol and has import which is something like meaning, so it makes a logical abstraction, but not in the familiar way of *genuine* symbols.[34] (My emphasis.)

Well, this indeed is caution to the point of withdrawal.

To an extent, then, Langer's preoccupation with the 'unconsummated' symbol represents a sidestep – albeit an unsuccessful one – from the present challenge. She disputes that the emotions 'presented' to us in music can be identified and located among the familiar everyday emotions; but in response to the natural requests

for the point or the importance of such expressiveness she merely
stipulates that connections between them must exist; though since
the emotions themselves are ineffable, it follows fairly directly that
the links must be also. Nevertheless, Langer seems to take it for
granted that these by now rather nebulous presentational emotions are given, as it were, on tap. Yet if we recall her images of
'tension and relaxation', 'flowing and stowing', we can see that
even this assumption is doubtful. For the point of such talk is
precisely that the images are indeed images – the description is
already figurative. Therefore even to talk about the tension in a
musical figure, be it harmonic or melodic, is already to make a
reading.

Compare this passage by the former critic Frank Howes, in
which he considers the finale of Sibelius's Second Symphony in an
attempt to locate musical emotion among the more familiar kinds:

> The change to D major with a prominent major third supervenes
> on a long piling up of D minor. Here the tonality of D minor is
> asserted as strongly as possible by scale passages running up
> and down ostinato fashion, and then with the F sharp the whole
> situation changes and reveals how great the relief is after tension
> (but not what caused the tension), how clear the certainty after
> doubt (but not what was in doubt), how triumphant is the issue
> of the struggle (but not what the struggle has been about nor
> who were struggling), how bright after dark (but not what
> caused the eclipse), and so on for any programme you might like
> to read into it. Plainly some experience gave rise to this musical
> change and some emotional experience must be read into it, just
> as it would be impossible to imagine that the proposition that
> two plus two equals four could have been discovered if no one
> had ever added two things to two other things.[35]

This is an illuminating passage in many ways. For the move from
entirely reasonable conjectures about possible programmes to
some 'plainly' emotional experience is a good illustration of the
grip that the emotion account has on the imagination of the
music-listening public. A moment's thought shows that there need
be no connection whatever between the ability of a musical
passage to sustain a particular image and some underlying experience on the part of the composer. To begin with, we can all depict
or refer to things that we have never experienced – our vocabulary

is larger than our life. Secondly, if the connection is to be at all interesting – that is, more than the purely trivial and general connection that someone must have experienced something in order for emotion to be expressed in music – it is always open to historical falsification, as we pointed out earlier. Howes clearly has this more ambitious connection in mind as he later remarks: 'The experiences of which this change is an abstract are plainly emotional',[36] ruling out the supposition that the experiences referred to were themselves merely abstracts or emblems. Howes, then, is the victim of sheer fixation, without regard to the coherence of his subsequent account.

Howes's writing is illuminating in another way, however – this time more valuable for my purposes. He makes it explicit that the emotional programme is 'read in' to the music by us, the listeners. And this admission alone makes the story about the composer's nervous system an unnecessary and misleading adjunct. What counts is that we read in not some fanciful item of biography, but an aspect under which we decide to hear the music, be it an aspect of conflict, obscurity or suffering. When we talk in this way, therefore, our reading of the musical work, our understanding, is already in business: we are already using images. And once again this demonstrates that no appeal to the emotions featuring in that figurative language can play any part of an explanation of the nature of the reading process.

Perhaps we can now see what is so misleading about the further aspect of Langer's analysis, namely the doctrine that the logical forms, or 'morphologies', of the musical figure and the emotion it is held to express, are in some way similar. The quest for that similarity, the enterprise of distilling the form of the music and of the emotional template is itself dependent on a prior reading of the work, bringing it under an aspect. We could not embark on such a quest without this bringing of the music under an aspect. Thus it is misleading to suppose that the form of an emotion somehow suggests itself to us as a result of similarities with the form of the music. The logical form is itself already parasitic on imagery: the idea of 'form' in this connection is already a metaphor. For this reason I return again to my motto, that the appeal to emotion, even at this most general and abstract level, cannot be explanatory of our understanding of music – since an understanding is already under way in such an appeal.

I shall round off this glance at the 'presentational' sense of emotion terms with a final complaint – namely that such terms are too frequently trivial. This complaint is in part empirical and in part philosophical. For anyone who is at all familiar with a given tradition of music can understand the application of emotion terms to music. Everyone knows what a sad tune is. We can all recognise them when we hear them; we have been told what they are like. I say 'told what they are like' deliberately, for it seems to me that this is true. In serious music no less than in pop music, we are instructed at an early age that this or that kind of tune is a sad or happy kind of tune. Indeed, 'sad' and 'happy' are frequently the explanation of the relation between the minor and major modes (rather than modes being used to explain the terms). Standardly this has nothing to do with any actual emotion being involved. Certain features just are, by agreement, features of sad and of happy tunes; we know what to look for in advance. In the popular music industry, fortunes are made by the simple application of basic formulae to produce sad tunes, which will be universally recognised as such, universally associated with equally formulaic types of lyrics, universally purchased, and universally rotated at the specified r.p.m.

And the situation is little, if any, better with serious music. The so-called anguish of diminished approaches to false cadences, or of the tension of suspended harmonies and piled-up dominants, have about as much to do with real anguish as the sad pop tune has to do with real sadness. These are codified ways of talking that tell us nothing. Such expressions are too true to be good. They give us no insight just because they do not surprise us, do not throw any light on the complexion of the music. They are not so much descriptive as prescriptive. The least competent listener can identify tormented music, can spot the tension in overlapping dominants and so on – even if he could not use a technical vocabulary in his descriptions. Of course in a sense that is just what he would be using, because the principal emotion terms have become precisely that – technical terms. They are effectively extensions of genuine emotion terms, applied in specifiable and checkable ways to specifiable features of the musical composition.

Now it will be objected at this point that even if I am right, such terms have only become technical from some other, prior and more interesting status. Otherwise why should this way of talking have been so attractive as to attain its present ubiquity? Weren't people originally struck by the evident links between certain first order features of the music, such as minor modes, rising sixths, and falling stepwise motion on the one hand, and the pattern of human sadness on the other?

The objection is a fair one at this particular stage, but not harmful to my overall contention. It is clear, of course, that emotion terms must in their first springtime flush have had a good deal of metaphorical point, exactly as do many other kinds of aspect descriptions today. Here the burden of explanation lies upon the musical work. But in any event, these connections between the first order features of the work and the patterns of human emotion are unlikely to be the connections that can any longer give rise to insight. Such descriptions do not alert us to more imaginative listening – on the contrary their very staleness can be an evasion of a more acute attention to the music. These descriptions have in a sense become part of our interpretative vocabulary – part of the background.

It is the ability to predict what these kinds of music will be like which, in my view, gives the game away. For if the sadness of many sad tunes has been reduced to this technical, manipulable level – as I maintain it has – then its metaphorical power has been dissipated, and its capacity for the stimulation of insight has been expended.

A few years ago, a Cardiff cinema swallowed hard and screened a film by the name of – I think this is right – *The Last Snows of Spring.* It was announced in the press that this was going to be a weepie, so the queues for the opening couple of nights were composed more or less exclusively of teenage girls, crying in advance of seeing the film. This remarkable piece of collective prophesy was reported on the local television news and the queues were subsequently swollen still further, as indeed were the cataracts of corporate salty tears that washed along Queen Street. But it was not clear what these tears had to do with sadness.

I turn now to the question of the affective sense of emotion, that sense in which we talk of the disturbances in our own mental and psychological states arising, sometimes legitimately, from our encounters with music. It seems perfectly reasonable to be moved by a particularly exciting or intense work, interpretation or performance – but equally reasonable not to be so moved. And by 'reasonable' I mean here that one could have a perfectly valid claim to have understood the musical enterprise, even at a very intense level, without having had certain feelings. Equally we could not have proved our understanding of the music by claiming to have had those feelings. We have said enough already to distinguish the listener who is moved incidentally, from the listener who abuses the music for its somatic effects on his nervous system. The question therefore is whether it is in any sense important to have been moved incidentally, in the course of listening. Popular answers have been in the affirmative, but have been over-zealously applied. For instance, writers have drawn analogies with the ability to see the point of jokes, inferring, and from the connections between such understanding and physical manifestations such as laughing and smiling, that understanding music has its natural manifestations in certain feelings. While this could be a helpful analogy, it is easy to see how harmful it may be if taken too seriously. For the purpose of humour is precisely to produce mirth; and to this extent if a poker-faced comedian can stimulate only poker faces in his audience, then he has failed. Despite the obvious intellectual content of nearly all humour, the enterprise is primarily somatic: we enjoy humour because laughter is the best medicine, and the production of laughter is its legitimate and primary task. But in the case of art, this is the whole point in contention. It is simply not the case that the purpose of art is cathartic or psychological, albeit by intellectually respectable methods. The business of art is more like the conveying of new points of view on the world, the enlarging of our consciousness. And this is shown, not in certain feelings which we may or may not have, but in subsequent things we do, say, listen to, play.

The identification of peculiar 'aesthetic' emotions, and the construing of emotion as the basis of understanding, in the doctrine of emotivism, seem to me to represent the most damaging results of the fascination for art as a means of producing feelings. I think the single mistake most responsible for isolating some queer aesthetic emotion is again the over-zealous application of a legitimate criterion; this time the criterion that the response to a piece of music be directed at, or intentional towards that music. Put simply, the criterion of directedness is that our response to music be distinguished from a somatic response only if it is characterised essentially by reference to the music itself. If, the argument runs, the response could be characterised entirely independently from the music then the connection between the music and the response might be simply causal; the response might have been obtained from some other stimulus. Well, this is familiar enough.

The trouble arises in the way we interpret 'independently characte-rised'. For example, one might argue like this: In referring to a work, one necessarily also refers to what it expresses, in that each is a function of the other. If we respond to an art-object, our response is tied to the object such that it could not separately be conceived, let alone characterised. For example, if my response to a given art-object is one of sadness, then the exact or peculiar quality of the sadness is determined only by immediate reference to the art-object itself. Thus what is important about the response is not the general concept of sadness, but the particular differentiation of sadness in this case. But that of course cannot be given indepen-dently. Again, if I attempt to specify my response in more detail, claiming an autumnal, wistful, cut-adrift quality to the sadness, then again what differentiates even this more singular description from a hundred other instances of using those exact words (and who can dispute that they might be so used on other occasions?) is the peculiar way in which they are informed by this particular art-object. And so each level of characterisation falls because by comparison with the art-object it remains hopelessly general. For example, this difficulty is brought out by R. G. Collingwood, in his *The Principles of Art*, though whether he himself avoids it is another matter:

> 'Expressing' emotions is certainly not the same thing as arousing them. There is emotion there before we express it. But as we express it, we confer upon it a different kind of emotional colouring; in one way, therefore, expression *creates what it expresses*, for exactly this emotion, colouring and all, *only exists so far as it is expressed* . . . we cannot say what 'emotion' is, except that we mean by it the kind of thing which, on the kind of occasion we are talking about, is expressed.[37]   (My emphasis.)

It should be clear what the view amounts to, namely that the art-object expresses what it expresses, and that my response is . . . my response. Any attempt to give a verbal characterisation is therefore made to look like an attempt to escape to an unacceptable level of generality.

Of course it is perfectly reasonable to ask someone to describe his response to a piece of music in a way that would break this trivial circle. Evidently this is simply a matter of applying the directedness criterion more sensibly. A smile is ultimately charac-

terised – indeed identified – only by a tacit reference to some
particular Cheshire cat or other, unless we are speaking of smiles
in general (which after all presuppose particular smiles). But no
one would suppose that the smile and the cat could not be
mentioned separately, nor described separately for ordinary purposes. Neither would we say it was nonsensical or futile to ask
what kind of an expression the cat is now wearing. The answer
might not, after all, always be 'a smile'. What we do is read the
expression, approaching the cat – or the piece of music – ready
prepared with a framework of possible judgements, apprehensions
and anticipations which have arisen from our wider experience of
Cheshire cats – and pieces of music – in general.

Roger Scruton, in his *Art and Imagination*, deals with the criterion
of directedness in a more elaborate manner. He acknowledges the
criterion (as he must) but disputes that it need be fulfilled by
making the piece of music the object necessarily of either judgements or beliefs. In fact, he argues that the kinds of response
appropriate to art-objects are essentially contrasted with beliefs
and with the judgements in which beliefs find expression. Instead,
the response is 'directed' at imaginative constructions, more or less
deliberately arrived at, bringing the art-object under this or that
aspect. A better way of putting it would be to say that the
imaginative constructions amount to different ways of attending to
the art-object (in Scruton's parlance, different modes of interest in
the art-object). He accepts that the aesthetic experience must be
described partly in terms of a perception of the art-object (fulfilling
the criterion of directedness), but he claims that the degree to
which the modes of interest are essentially up to us, the listeners,
drives the necessary wedge between the criterion of directedness
on the one hand, and the essential vacuity of the response which
has no independent characterisation whatever, on the other.
Scruton cites humour and fantasy as examples of attitudes towards
wholly imaginary objects, and points out that these constitute
'modes of interest' in objects which are securely divorced from
belief. The burden of his account then falls on imagination, which
he treats separately. Well, this seems an interesting, fresh and
competent account which I believe to be right thus far; it would
therefore stand or fall by the degree of success of his theory of
imagination. Once again, then, the mistake to which I referred, of
being over-zealous in applying the directedness criterion, is seen
as a mistake – that is, something that can and should be avoided.

Of course it is my complaint that the mistake has not always been avoided, but has rather led aestheticians to posit the aesthetic response as being essentially emotional in character, doubtless involving beliefs about the object of the emotion – the trouble being that since the emotions are logically tied to their objects in the strongest sense, they can never be characterised, owing to the acutely high degree of differentiation among different art-objects. If each art-object is, as it were, *sui generis*, it must follow that the corresponding emotion is also *sui generis*. And indeed, the art-object always is held on these accounts to be unique, unrepeatable, defined of itself. Of course it follows once again from this that the aesthetic emotion is ineffable – ultimately nothing can be said of it other than that one has it at the time of the having. This account needs merely to be stated in order to be dismissed; yet it emerges even in recent writing, such as this, from Hepburn's examination of emotional qualities, setting out the distinction of the aesthetic emotion from emotions more generally:

> Emotions, agitations, feelings of various kinds get themselves named only when there is some utilitarian point in their having names – particularly if they tend to recur frequently in ordinary human experience. But, as we earlier reminded ourselves, art deals very little in the repetitive and the stereotyped. Its slant on the world is often in striking contrast to that of workaday utility. The probability, then, is that its emotions should show the same contrast: their namelessness is no argument for their non-existence.[38]

Perhaps it is not such an argument; however, it does seem an argument for their vacuity.

Taken further, I think we can see how the concern with the directedness criterion leads to a temptation to conflate emotion and understanding. This conflation is crystallised in the doctrine of emotivism, namely that understanding a work of art consists in having certain feelings, certain quite special, art-orientated feelings that are available only to those of the utmost sensitivity (as we gathered earlier from the passage from Fry's *Vision and Design*). There are two parallel ways in which this mistake might come to be made.

Firstly, I think we can see in the way Wollheim attempted to bridge the gap between how things were with him, and how they were with the art-object (via hypothetical claims about how things might be with other minds) a kind of argument from analogy. If he could establish, however tenuously, some sort of affective emotion in the spectator/listener, this could constitute a kind of warrant for things we might be able to say about the presentational emotions in an art-object, and, through them, about the sorts of affects in a composer or writer which might tend to result in the production of this sort of work. Again, the crudity of this exposition should not distract us from its essential faithfulness to Wollheim's visible enterprise. Now like other arguments from analogy, this one won't work, and we have discussed its failure in depth. A parallel exists, however, in the 'nameless', ineffable, *sui generis* 'aesthetic emotion'. If (a big 'if') it is indeed produced in the competent listener, then by analogy it gives the insight into what the composer was trying to express (remembering the while that this too is nameless). There must be at least an unconscious temptation to follow this path.

Secondly, the modern analysis of emotion as being essentially evaluative must bear some blame for the continuing temptation towards an emotivist view. This comes out in Ronald Hepburn's efforts to rescue some kind of explanatory status for emotions, in the article already mentioned:

Recent philosophical analyses of emotion concepts have shown that when, for instance, we say 'A feels remorse', 'B is indignant', 'C is bitter', we do something far more complex than claim A and B behave in certain identifiable ways and experience types of inner turmoil ... concepts like 'remorse', 'indignation' give interpretations of a situation, interpretations that go beyond the recording of acts and feelings occurring at any particular moment. 'C feels bitter about the way he was treated' carries as part of its meaning 'C believes he OUGHT NOT to have been so treated', 'C believes he was treated BADLY'. That is, being bitter involves making certain evaluations, not simply having feelings or acting in particular ways. Traditional accounts of emotion used to give central place to determinate, recognisable *feelings* – inner and private. .... The current opinion refuses to give pride of place to such feelings, and (in the case of some writers) denies even the *existence* of feelings specific to particular emotions. Instead their analyses are given in terms of situation-appraisals plus an undifferentiated general excitation.[39]

Again we see that by concentrating on the cognitive aspects of a process in which emotion might elsewhere be a feature, namely the process of situation-appraisal, we can soon make emotion appear to be 'evaluative'. The trick lies in quietly forgetting that the emotion is no longer the linch-pin. Hepburn, just like Wollheim in his talk about 'feedback from judgement', is making the tail wag the dog. It is not emotion which is responsible for the evaluation, but judgement. Emotion is a response to the judgements, although so concurrently wedded to it that in familiar cases – say, fear of the dentist – it might appear to be the form which the evaluation takes. But to say that fear is our response, is not to say that fear is our evaluation, or that fear is our judgement. Rather our fear shows what our judgement *is*. It is easy to see how a mistake could sustain the myth that having a peculiar feeling on hearing a work is what constitutes insight into that work. When I listen to the 'Quoniam' from the *Missa Solemnis* I do often get a feeling akin almost to vertigo. Signally, this does not deter my return to the music. It might be true that I could not get that particular feeling without listening to the music, or without imagining it in the mind's ear. Yet the feeling arises, if at all, from an understanding, from a set of judgements. In seeking to account for the judgements, I set the feeling aside.

There are two other difficulties with the emotivist position which are worth recording – both will be familiar to students of ethics. First, disagreement in aesthetics could amount on this thesis only to a squabble over who genuinely has the 'peculiar feeling'. But such feelings, as we have already noted, are self-authenticating. Hence disputes are not merely insoluble, they cannot coherently arise. Thus the emotivist view entails that all critical disagreement is a mistake, the waving in the darkness of cudgels that could never collide. Equally, all criticism must be ultimately futile, for if it cannot correct the view of another, it is hard to see how it could help him at all.

Second, absolutely anything could count as an aesthetic response to an art-object provided only that it was directed towards, or intentional in regard to the art-object. Thus if I habitually smoke my pipe when I hear the *Nimrod* variation, no one could ever prove to me that this was not a legitimately aesthetic response; for I could always claim that it was the inevitable manifestation of a feeling. The same would be true if I rolled my eyes at the 'Golliwog's Cake Walk', or clutched at my brow during 'And With

His Stripes We Are Healed'. All I would ever need to do would be to claim (and self-deception has a field-day here) that my response was essentially directed at the music in question. The consequences for the whole area of aesthetics are that, being boundless, it simply collapses as an identifiable discourse. For if just anything can be an aesthetic response, then in any important sense nothing can.

I have been concerned to limit the place of emotion to an accompaniment or an expression, rather than a constituent, of our understanding of music. But I have admitted that predicates applied to music in other than their primary sense include emotion terms as important and familiar candidates. What I argue is that the explanation of such terms is just a part of a more general explanation of metaphors, comparisons and aspect descriptions. It is to the beginning of such an explanation that I now turn.

Notes

1. Susanne Langer, *Feeling and Form* (Routledge & Kegan Paul, 1953), p. 28.
2. Ibid.
3. Richard Wagner, *A Happy Evening* (*Abend Zeitung*, Dresden, 1841).
4. Franz Liszt, *Die Zigeuner und ihre Musik in Ungarn* (1861), p. 332.
5. I owe this example to Dr R. A. Sharpe.
6. Deryck Cooke, *The Language of Music* (Oxford University Press, 1953), p. 33.
7. Antony Hopkins, *Talking about Sonatas* (Heinemann, 1971), p. 123.
8. Roger Fry, *Vision and Design* (Chatto & Windus, 1925), p. 15.
9. *Langer*, op. cit., p. 27.
10. Richard Wollheim, *Art and its Objects* (Peregrine, Penguin, 1975), p. 38.
11. Ibid., p. 49.
12. Ibid.
13. Susanne Langer, *Philosophy in a New Key* (Harvard University Press, 1951), p. 217.
14. Huw Morris-Jones, 'The Language of Feeling', *Br. J. Aesthetics*, Vol. 2, 1962, 18.
15. Wollheim, *Art and its Objects*, p. 39.
16. Eduard Hanslick, *The Beautiful in Music* (Novello, reprint of 1891 translation), pp. 26–7.
17. Wollheim, *Art and its Objects*, p. 40.
18. Ibid., p. 46.
19. Ibid., p. 47.
20. Ibid., p. 48.

21. Ibid.
22. André Previn and Antony Hopkins, *Music Face to Face* (Hamish Hamilton, 1971), p. 89.
23. Bojan Bujic, 'Aesthetics of Music', *Br. J. Aesthetics*, Vol. 15, 1975.
24. Ronald Hepburn, 'Emotions and emotional qualities: some attempts at analysis', *Br. J. Aesthetics*, Vol. 1, 1961, 256.
25. Ibid., p. 257.
26. Ibid.
27. Ibid., p. 258.
28. Ibid., p. 256.
29. Langer, *Feeling and Form*, p. 27.
30. Langer, *Philosophy in a New Key*, p. 244.
31. Susanne Langer, 'Expressiveness', in *Problems of Art* (Routledge & Kegan Paul, 1957), pp. 25–6.
32. Langer, *Philosophy in a New Key*, p. 244.
33. Langer, *Problems of Art*, p. 240.
34. Ibid., p. 127.
35. Frank Howes, *Music and its Meanings* (University of London, 1958), p. 29.
36. Ibid., pp. 29–30.
37. R. G. Collingwood, *The Principles of Art* (Oxford University Press, 1938), p. 152.
38. Hepburn, 'Emotions', p. 263.
39. Ibid., p. 260.

3

Judgement

We often speak of the interpretation of music as if it were basically something that is done by performers, but this is a misleading view. All of us who listen to music with any direction in our listening, who understand what we hear in terms of direction, sequence and purpose, are necessarily interpreting what we hear. When we are satisfied or dissatisfied by a particular performance of a piece of music, we are, like the performer, engaged in a process of judgement, evaluation and interpretation of the items in the musical text. In this sense the distinction between performer and listener is considerably less marked than we might ordinarily suppose. Of course in a certain sense the listener depends on the performer, but it seems to me that the performer actuates a process of listening in which both he and audience engage. What the performer does is to occasion, and to channel, the listening of his audience, who remain free to disagree with what he does. Usually a performer will have taken the trouble to achieve a more intense involvement with the music than will a typical member of his audience, but this need by no means be necessarily the case.

We may justifiably regard a performance as an *occasion* of listening – a peg on which thoughts are hung, arranged and compared. We both listen to what a performer does, and listen through it. For when we listen to a piece of music it is not the case, except only in a very attenuated sense, that the music is made available to us through that performance. This is shown by the fact that we can compare and contrast different performances of the same work. It would be more true to say that music is made available to us amid, and by the agency of our own imaginations. As we listen we engage in a complicated process of retention and comparison. The performer may invite certain quite specific comparisons between this phrase and that, between this movement and another, but we always remain free to accept or reject this invitation in favour of one which we prefer.

In even the simplest musical activity, such as following a tune, we are retaining, comparing and contrasting successive tones and assembling the shape of the melody in our own imaginations. In comparing phrases or whole movements we are building upon this technique. As such we are already involved in an act of interpretation. In being listeners at all, we are in a sense already critics. Of course we may articulate our critical faculties in different ways. We may express our choices and preferences simply by inclining to hear the phrase played in a certain way (such as by playing or singing it that way ourselves) or we may simply habitually play the recording of a favourite performance. As Wittgenstein suggests,[1] our tendency to act like this remains the first criterion of our preferences. But we should always be able to explain and support our preferences by verbal judgements, and the kind of reasons we give for those choices may well make sense to others, and command their assent. Indeed, if we consider how we learn to refine our own listening, this is perhaps one of the most important ways in which we enlarge and intensify our own conceptions of a piece of music. And it remains true that verbal judgements are the most central and prevalent means of expressing our understanding of music. And for this reason I want to try and examine the way we use verbal judgements to express that understanding.

We can, it is true, often illuminate what we say by actual musical notes, but usually the substance of our understanding must be conveyed verbally, if only to give a context to the illumination. The process of criticism then may begin in sound, but it is brought to fruition in words. Our understanding of what we hear is, to a large extent, identified by what we say. So our task is to examine the language of critical judgement, and to account for our ability to understand and to engage in it.

The critic often uses two sorts of language, but these are usually fused together intimately. They are necessarily two faces of a coin. On the one face we see the critic using the language of the analyst, cutting into the musical text to expose its technical components and their relationships. The emphasis which a performer gives to these components is often a matter for critical scrutiny. On the other face the critic uses the language of the poet; for by the use of image and metaphor he calls our attention to a way of listening which might defy prescription by technical analysis alone. The critic – and here by 'critic' I mean anyone who is fortunate enough to share in a discourse about a musical work with other listeners – identifies and expresses his own imaginative activity, and commends it to us. He invites us to use our imaginations in the way that he has used his. Just as the poet both expresses and commends the intervention of his imagination into the affairs which he examines, so the critic of a piece of music or of a performance, in using language which is figurative rather than descriptive, persuasive rather than, perhaps, informative, conveys and commends the intervention of his imagination into the musical events which he examines.

The first of these two kinds of language – the language of the analyst – is the concern of the musical textbook (in which context alone will the total separation of the two kinds of language be readily found). The 'rudiments of music' are, properly speaking, the rudiments of analysis and not of listening as a whole. The identifiable and separable parts of the musical text form the subject matter of a reasonably exact discipline.

The second of these two kinds of language – the language of the poet – is the concern of a philosophical inquiry. The grammar of this kind of language involves the grammar of metaphor, and it is accordingly part of our job to look at how metaphors operate. The images of a particular reading of a musical text often seem to be the most illuminating part of that reading, and yet they seem not to be open to the independent scrutiny of a textbook analysis in the way that the conventionally described components of the musical structure are. They seem, furthermore, to be logically tied to what the individual listener brings to the music and can therefore be commended only within the terms of an actual experience of listening. But as I shall argue they are not thereby so irreducibly personal as to resist explanation, nor need they avoid being tested. For the concept of there being more and less appropriate images requires that we can indeed test them.

Furthermore, these two kinds of language are interdependent. For criticism which confined itself to structural analysis would seem to tell us very little about the value or importance of a particular work or interpretation. But by corollary, criticism which confined itself solely to a series of images might fail to locate the items of the experience which it expressed within an understanding of the work as a coherent whole. In other words, it is difficult to see what *importance* a piece of structural analysis could have for a listener who was unwilling to bring his imagination to bear on the musical text. Yet by corollary it is difficult to see what *coherence* could attach to the images offered by someone from whom the relations within the component parts of the musical structure were concealed.

The way that critical judgements work is best seen through examples. In trying to understand what is involved in the following extracts, I want to try and find out in each case what the critic is bringing to the music and what he wants to convey and commend to us – and to see how he achieves this in his judgements.

In my first example, Wilfrid Mellers discusses the A minor Fugue from Book I of Bach's *Well-Tempered Clavier*:

> The passage is at once exciting and frightening. The last two bars, returning to the diminished segment of the theme and its thrusting trills, dam the flood as though by a conscious act of will, and with an almost triumphant foot-stamping. . . . The A minor (fugue) is the most unambiguously physical of the fugues in the '48' though its physicality threatens to blow up and embrace 'other modes of experience that may be possible'.[2]

Secondly, Josef Weingarten, in an essay entitled 'Interpreting Schumann's piano music', sets out his prescriptions for the approach to playing Schumann's earlier compositions:

> Early compositions such as the Abegg variations, Papillons, Carnaval, Kinderscenen, are all a series of miniatures strung together like beads on a necklace to form a single chain. Here the dedicated performer has problems to solve. Each miniature is complete within itself, with its own particular musical structure, tempo and atmosphere. Moreover they vary in length, and it is this richness and variety of musical imagination which give them their perennial appeal and fascination for both performer and audience. For the former there is the added excitement of giving to each cameo its own distinctive qualities which have to be captured instantaneously and incorporated into the whole: any change of approach during the playing will distort the whole picture. But it is not enough to produce a series of perfect miniatures. For both in spite and because of their contrasts they are facets of a whole. Unless this unity is apparent, the pieces will dissolve into brilliant fragments like mercury and lose their continuity or, where the pieces are of opposing style and tempo, of contrast. Each pause both links and separates, and has to be

just long enough to allow the listener (and this includes the player) to gain a complete impression of one miniature before his interest becomes involved in its equally enchanting neighbour.[3]

And thirdly, Neville Cardus eulogises – as who would not? – over the playing of Vladimir Horowitz in concert:

> His playing of Scarlatti ... was so finely shaped and delicate of texture that it would have broken into powdered glass had a single false overpressed touch fallen on its crystal surface.[4]

The first of these passages occurs in what I might call programmed analysis. Mellers has a visible enterprise, that of demonstrating a vein of religious celebration running through Bach's music – including apparently detached instrumental works like the 'forty-eight'. Mellers has a programmatic axe to grind, and he grinds it, subsequently to the quoted passage, on the gritwheel of fairly close textual analysis of his chosen works. He is openly searching for a specific aspect in the music he selects, and he gears his analysis to exposing that aspect, and to drawing our attention to the music in such a way that we too will find plausible that impetus which he believes to be covertly present. In short, then, Mellers has a precise reading of the music in question, and his judgements, and the language in which they are expressed, are aimed at securing our approval – indeed, our sharing – of that reading. Consequently, in the passage I have quoted we can find two strands of persuasion: firstly the challenge of the extended metaphor of 'energy in spate' running throughout the extract and expressed in convinced and committed language; and secondly a direct appeal to mysticism via the quotation referring to 'enlarged modes of experience'. But this latter is simply an unargued assertion – a claim directly lodged – and has no practical interest for us. It is the process of persuasion via the image which interests me, and on which I shall enlarge.

Weingarten's recipe for the approach to performing Schumann's piano miniatures is also a piece of propaganda in that he too has a visible enterprise of persuading us to approve and adopt the kind of approach he himself favours (not surprisingly, since his essay is after all a didactic work). However, Weingarten is not concerned with close textual analysis as such. Indeed, he seems to regard each piece as individually exempt from analysis, each taking its force and perhaps even its sense from a kind of *gestalt* to which all contribute. This is very much a pianist talking about the imaginative and conceptual preparation for playing, and what he has to say about the musical pause has a quite general value and application. But once again, the main vehicle of his writing is an extended image of sparkling and discrete beads or droplets. He commends to us his particular intervention in the music through a hard image.

Thirdly, I included the remark of Neville Cardus as an instance of a critic (in the more formal sense) doing what he is paid to do: going to hear music performed and telling us what he heard. Again, the principal power of what he says arises from the metaphor which he employs – one which I personally find extraordinarily persuasive. The phrase 'crystal surface' in a sense actualises rather than merely amplifies the preceding image. The impression of both the poise of Scarlatti's writing, and the delicacy of Horowitz's control, is transmitted to us with intensity, and with relish.

I do not claim that these are typical examples of critical writing; indeed I am not certain how we could identify such examples. But the passages I have quoted are important in that they are clearly distinct from the kind of writing that informs us, on the one hand, that the leap to the submediant appears in disguised form four times in a single climax, or on the other hand that Haydn was undoubtedly a happy man and Beethoven's D major Piano Sonata op. 28, is 'about' walking in his favourite stretch of woodland.

The writers are all aware of the items of the musical text and the first two writers refer to these items in the course of advocating the position to which they are committed. Each has 'read' what he hears, rather in the way that we speak of 'reading' a situation. And so the judgements to which these readings give rise are our central interest.

The questions naturally arising with such judgements might be these: how much of our reading stems from the items of the musical text presented to us, and how much from our own personal histories – the connections, associations and contrasts which we naturally bring to the music? Moreover, can we legitimately distinguish between these two sources? Are there really independent 'given' and indisputable items of musical experience, on which our imaginations subsequently operate? Or does the very identity of the musical text depend in some sense on our making some reading or other? (the familiar question of idealism).

Assuming the distinction, between the given and what we supply, to be a valid one, what part does the recognition of 'given' features play in our reading? How naturally does a musical text bear the images which we subsequently impose on it – and, for that matter, is there any limit to the number of intelligible interpretations? Taken collectively, these questions invite an account of the grounds of our judgements, and furthermore of the grounds of their being understood and shared by others. And such an account is therefore the goal of the present chapter and of its successors.

I think that we can take the case of melody as an instructive model of the way we might proceed. Melody, unaccompanied and isolated, is the simplest form of tonal organisation. I would discount rhythms here because the items in a rhythm need no tonal value. Now, tunes are obviously not self-labelling; the sequences of tones which constitute tunes are heard as such, have a sense and a direction, only for those who are listening in the right kind of way. The listener must be anticipating and assessing and retaining the direction and value of each interval, adding each to its predecessors, and modifying any expectations of its successors and, simultaneously with the unfolding of the tune, assembling a kind of synthesis. Indeed, a little thought shows that this must also be true of a single isolated interval, which must be heard and understood as such, rather than simply heard. In a similar way, the non-tonal components of a rhythm must also be apprehended and assembled by the listener; the strokes in a rhythm are related, but only for someone who is in a position to relate them. Consequently, melody and rhythm are heard as melody and rhythm only by someone who is master of a particular technique – which has to be learned, developed and applied. It is no objection to point out the unconscious fluency with which this trick is usually performed – for we are good at it simply through long practice. Indeed there are occasions when we have to exercise the technique with some considerable conscious effort, as we listen to less accessible tunes (even to speak of the 'accessibility' of a tune reveals what the listener must for his own part be contributing). 'Easy listening' is, as it were, no idle phrase.

Now it seems to me that something like this process is involved at higher levels of tonal organisation, and indeed in the bringing of what we hear under non-musical, figurative descriptions, as I intend to show. And we can in any case begin immediately to apply ourselves to the questions which we thought to arise over judgements in general. Let us direct these questions to our hearing of a melody as a melody. The grounds of such hearing must lie in a technique into which we are inducted, and in which we become fluent. Nevertheless, we are inclined to hear tunes at all because certain sequences of tones invite the description 'melody' very readily; others less so, and still others not at all. Indeed the existence of a melody will usually be a matter of the express intention of someone or other, although this need not always be so. We could hear melody in the random clankings within a boiler factory, because we ourselves are supplying the synthesis within which a melody comes to be heard as such. But of course it is unlikely that our general conception of melody could ever have arisen in so haphazard a way, and any general account of melody must incorporate an acknowledgement of this purposive direction within any melody, thereby distributing the grounds of our understanding of melody between the notes themselves and our hearing of them. In general terms the listener and the melody stand in a kind of mutual dependence, for not only would there be no listeners if there were no melody, it is difficult to see how we could describe or identify melody if there were no listeners. In this way we dismiss the idealist threat that melody exists only in the mind of the person hearing it, yet at the same time acknowledge the fairly wide community of listeners who, taken collectively, give coherence and identity to melodies in general. Ultimately it is through being part of such a community of what we might call agreement in melody that we understand and hear melody. We participate in a technique that is shared among many. And there is more than one technique – our familiar diatonic basis for melody is not the only such basis.

In the same way, our understanding of more highly differentiated musical organisations, and of the judgements which express or refer to them, is grounded in a participation in more highly differentiated techniques. Many people share the recognition of, and discourse concerning, structure, counterpoint, development and variation, but not quite so many as can respond to a simple melody. They speak a more restricted and specialised vocabulary. And in characterising music according to the emotions it is said to express (or, less reputably, generate) we are speaking a kind of language that is current in a particular circle of understanding – quite a wide one, as I argued in the last chapter. This too is a technique which we learn, and which is based on a grasp of the melodies and harmonies which, understood together, are said to give emotion judgements their application. The structures and the feelings they are held to express must be *read*; they are genuine or important for the listener only in so far as he himself discerns them and interprets the music in terms of them. We talk of structures, and we talk of feelings, because we have learned to do so in certain circumstances, and because we have learned to recognise when those situations have come about. We have learned to bring certain kinds of descriptions to bear on certain kinds of musical texts. And it is often satisfying for us to do so, and we need no further justifications than these.

What I wish to argue is that the reading of more elusive and perhaps more imaginative aspects in music – aspects which are much less accessible in the ordinary run of things – is nevertheless simply a yet more highly differentiated technique, understood and shared by others who play the same kind of game. They learn to look more keenly and more adventurously, for more sophisticated, diaphanous and fleeting kinds of things, and they learn to understand and to appreciate when others are doing this.

Indeed, I believe this represents the beginning, at any rate, of an account of judgements involving imagery, although we shall have to say more about the way metaphors function within these judgements. Yet whatever that operation, judgements involving them make sense within this circle of agreement about the value and point of using such kinds of description. This agreement is constituted by the shared commitment to certain kinds of objects and situations, music among them, that merit this special kind of attention; and it is constituted by the shared technique of bringing our imaginations to bear in certain intense and adventurous ways. We will tend to know what someone else is doing in applying poetic or figurative language, to the extent that we would know what we ourselves were doing with such language – although I hasten to add that the one is not a cause of the other. If we have succeeded in establishing the collective language, we need to look at how the processes involved actually operate, and this must sooner or later take us to an examination of metaphors themselves.

First, though, let us look at the process of recognition. To take Wilfrid Mellers's remarks about 'physicality' and 'foot-stamping', our recognition of these aspects in the music – if indeed we do recognise them – depends at least in part on a certain preparedness. We must, as it were, have a place ready in our imagination to be filled by the idea of the foot-stamping in the music. It is not enough simply to say that the music is of such and such a nature as to invite that particular image. To talk about the nature of the music in this way is simply to talk about the sorts of description that it will satisfactorily fulfil. But those descriptions may very well include the very description we are trying to explain. The most this could achieve would be to give us a paraphrase of the description at issue. In any event, these descriptions are themselves very largely a matter of agreement. We will be able to say, independently of hearing the actual A minor Fugue itself, what kind of musical features would suggest the phrase 'foot-stamping'; and our ability to do this will arise from our knowledge of many different examples of music that we have learned to characterise in certain ways, according to what is suggested by their vigour of tempo and measure, the predominance of rhythm over melody, or the opportunities given to the percussive instruments in the accompaniment, and so on. So to say that music is of this foot-stamping nature is simply to say that it is of an identifiable kind and that a whole family of descriptions will be variously agreed to by listeners who have learned to describe this kind of music as they have learned to describe many other kinds. In a very real sense, then, the particular ability of certain musical texts to satisfy certain sorts of description is, once the descriptions are current, basically a matter of our continuing collective willingness to use those descriptions. And that willingness is probably not a very interesting phenomenon at all. Indeed, much music may even be written with certain descriptions in mind, or not entirely absent from mind. Again to talk about 'physicality' is to suggest other related descriptions and to indicate certain quite specifiable features such as boisterous tempo, four-square structure and full-blooded instrumentation (even 'full-blooded' is here a family relative of 'physical').

So what I am saying is that recognition is not simply a passive attitude to what in some sense '*is*': rather it is a collectively understood judgement that we tend to make under certain kinds of circumstances. It is what we do and say when prompted that is interesting, rather than the prompting itself (which seems to me to be fairly trivial and readily described). Recognition implies something about the listener who recognises, as well as about the music which is recognised – under this or that description. And again, as in the case of melody, it is this duality which lays to rest the shade of the 'naive' listener, who threatens to bring nothing whatever to his listening, yet hopes to carry something away with him – a bargain indeed, were it possible, which it is not. If he brings nothing to his listening, then he can be surprised or satisfied by nothing; but this is simply to say that he does not listen at all, but merely hears noises. To talk about recognition at all is to talk about descriptions, and not about a private incursion (non-verbal) into the hearer's soul. The *occasion* for recognising an aspect – the prompting – is the music itself, but the *intelligibility* of the aspects recognised, their satisfaction of the musical text, rests on an agreement in description. And the *responsibility* for recognition lies with the listener.

Equally, then, if the question is reformulated in terms of what the music supplies and what we ourselves supply, the solution for any given description is reducible to this same dual relationship. And so the idea that interpretation takes us in some measure 'beyond the text' is misleading, for it seems to suggest that interpretation comes in only after the identity and composition of the musical text have been established. But that patently is not true, for even the textbook analysis kinds of terminology refer, like melody, to the fruit of an interpretative process, namely that of reading the melody, of hearing the sequences of tones under that description, however naturally it may appear to fall to our lips. And in practice these 'technical' descriptions occur in a state of intimacy with their 'non-technical' or 'figurative' or 'evaluative' colleagues. The difference between judgements about parallel fifths or dominant sevenths, and judgements about 'beads on a necklace', is not that one kind is given and the other interpreted, but that one kind belongs to a vocabulary with one sort of currency and the other belongs to a vocabulary with a different sort of currency. Indeed, it is arguable which of these two particular kinds of judgement is more current or widespread. We tend to think of textbook analysis as being the province of a few academics, which to an extent it is, yet is not something similar true of the more penetrating, incisive and adventurous images that those who are most intensely involved with a particular work will fly at one another? For in many cases the two kinds of understanding will be inseparable to the extent that they will need to be current amongst the same circle of listeners. And indeed the three examples of writing that I have quoted seem to me to deploy images that depend on the intermingling of both these sorts of vocabulary.

An obvious objection to this account is that terms like 'melody', 'harmony', 'structure' and so forth, have the kind of application that can be tested – often conclusively. And perhaps expressions such as 'beads on a necklace' used in a figurative sense do not have the benefit of such conclusive demonstrations. But I think the objection is superficial. For the great majority of images are understood precisely because they, too, are open to a kind of testing for their appropriateness in any given application. It may well be that the circle of people among whom such expressions are understood tends to become smaller as the image becomes more startling and more truly figurative. But some figurative language is sufficiently current to be regarded as straightforwardly descriptive quite as much as it is figurative. And most images may be tested for their appropriateness. This in itself shows that judgements involving such images are part of the same general technique that supports the discernment of melody, namely the technique of attending in an informed and directed way, under descriptions which are learned and grasped. To hear a sonata-form movement as a structure is to attend in a peculiarly informed way, which we can describe. And in the same way we are able to describe the kind of listening that must be done to hear a sequence of tones as a melody, or to hear the physicality in Bach's A minor Fugue, or to hear the crystal surface of Horowitz's playing of Scarlatti.

Figurative expressions are used in a sense other than their primary sense as straightforward descriptions, but this does not, of course, mean that they will not be perfectly well understood, and after a fashion testable for their appropriateness. Everyone knows what a battleaxe is and everyone knows what an 'old battleaxe' is (perhaps the latter claim is, if anything, more certain than the former). And consequently this non-primary sense of figurative expressions is no argument for supposing that figurative judgements are *ipso facto* any more interpreted than are, say, judgements about the strengths and weaknesses of a soccer team, or remarks about the consequences of bad weather.

It may again be objected that the power of the image used by, for instance, Neville Cardus in connection with Horowitz playing Scarlatti – namely the shattering of the crystal surface – so magnificently exceeds the capacity of such mundane images as 'old battleaxe' to arrest and startle, as to require a completely different analysis. And indeed there are images whose power seems to consist in their very inappropriateness (understood on one level); their capacity to arrest and startle us lies in the fact that they do not mingle with our ordinary descriptions but rather collide with them. In answer to this objection I intend to claim, and I hope to show, that even here their intelligibility is underpinned by something akin to a technique; it is here that my argument will require the further dimension of a more careful scrutiny of the function of a metaphor within judgements. But even without this aid, it seems clear that in order to be surprised by, as it were, the collision of ideas that do not belong together, some kind of preparedness on our part is essential. Again, I would like to draw on a comparison with melody. Sometimes, a pretty tune is transformed by a single pungent interval into a memorable statement. But it will be clear that this can be heard only by those doing the right kind of listening, namely, those who are anticipating differently. Furthermore, the capacity for surprise is not of itself sufficient, for we could be surprised by the ghastly interval that wrecked a good tune. Not just any 'wild' note can succeed; the arresting interval must make its own sense, and the surprise must be satisfying, and not bewildering. So the listener must be prepared for certain possibilities, but not for limitless ones. The essence of the surprise consists, perhaps, in being unpredictable, but not in being incoherent. And so it must be with images; for an image to be startling, it must remain appropriate, though perhaps appropriate when judged by standards which we had not foreseen. Perhaps, indeed, truly powerful images can be used only once, and their logic seen only retrospectively.

It seems that we are once again back to the duality between the expectations of a sufficiently sophisticated listener and the items of a musical text. The truly startling image will have its roots in both. What is peculiar about the explanation of such images is not the fact of their place within a 'language game' (in Wittgenstein's sense) but the kinds of shared assumptions and expectations which underpin it. These images are more nearly idiosyncratic, and they must work because the language game is more nearly idiosyncratic. But even idiosyncrasies have their explanation, and their role must always lie amidst the predictable, in contrast to which lies their power.

What of the experience of a passage of music, of which our judgements are essentially the expression? At the outset, it is obvious that our general practice of listening can be characterised in terms of experiences, and that these accumulate and that our learning the techniques of informed and committed listening occurs through the medium of individual listening experiences. It is, after all, through hearing music in conjunction with the judgements of others that we have learned to give those sorts of judgements ourselves. The total of our separate experiences of hearing music stands behind and informs the listening we do on any occasion now.

But inevitably the philosophical interest lies not here, but in the actuality of the particular experience of hearing music under this or that concept – the experience of bringing music under judgement. For if any of the experiences which formed our technique were important, then *this* one must be important now.

We listen to music at all because we find it in some sense important to do so, and any aesthetic situation has, in addition to a value, a kind of imperative about it that causes us to seek and return to it as well as to pronounce upon it. We value pieces of music, but we also value the individual experiences of listening to them. The question, In what does this value consist? must have an answer that is part philosophical and part psychological. For there is always the possibility that my devotion to any particular piece of music or even to a single phrase is explained by something from my unconscious. In our present enquiry we can do no more than acknowledge those reasons. Our philosophical task is to outline the conceptual links between the music and the experience of the listener. Interpreting music is not simply a matter of obediently fitting certain judgements to certain musical items as though we were fulfilling a pattern – a description which might seem to follow from the account I have given in terms of participating in a technique. It is more real than that, just as the punchline of a joke is more real than the conclusion of a syllogism.

I turn again to the case of melody for instruction. One reason that melody has the capacity to affect us might be that we invoke sets of half-formed connections with the rhythms and intonations of speech, with the rhythms and gestures of the body, and we discussed Richard Wollheim's steps down this path in the last chapter. On any given occasion these connections may be an empirical matter, susceptible to a straightforward testing.

Wittgenstein suggests that the intonations of language are important[5] while Langer inclines towards parallels with the way that we respond to workaday circumstances and situations.[6] However unclear and diffuse these things may be (and they are certainly unclear) some explanation embodying them seems bound to underly our psychological affiliation to melody. But there are two things to be said at once. First, this inevitably psychological story cannot of itself explain the grounds of our understanding of melody, but only our liability to be affected by it. (Which was, of course, the conclusion of the last chapter.) Secondly, the kind of melody that tends to produce this or that affect in us is actually largely a matter of agreement – a fact which seems to me to be of great significance, yet which has passed unremarked in most writing on the subject. Our idiosyncratic or psychological responses to certain melodic phrases occur within this more general agreement about what is, for example, a serene, wistful or poignant theme (and such general agreement is readily discoverable). Moreover, these general agreements will cover cases that might plausibly be explained by dark hints about the rhythm and intonation of language or of bodily gesture, and these are things which we learn about melody as we learn to listen to it – we learn what is expressive almost ostensively. So our central experience of melody – which is no doubt itself the important joy in our listening – rests on what we have learned to look for. Perhaps our satisfaction comes in part from the reassurance that is due to the skilled applications of our imagination to what we hear. How we hear rests on what we know.

This becomes clearer as we consider what it is to hear a specific aspect in a musical item. For example, I may hear a stony or gritty quality in the texture of a slow movement from a Haydn quartet. I might be able to support this description by drawing attention to other features of my experience of the music – the angular melodic line, the stubborn refusal of the accompaniment to accommodate shifting harmonies, and so on – all features of my experience of the music as a whole. I might point to the insistent rhythmic divisions that seem to undermine the tempo and contour of the melody; and such judgements inevitably express the music as it 'presents itself' to me – as I should want to say in such circumstances. In other words I will be directing the image that I use – that of stoniness – towards specific items in the musical text and I will be drawing attention to features of the music as I experience it. Now it is an important fact that I can often obtain the agreement of others to the descriptions that I give, and it is characteristic of my giving such descriptions that I desire such agreement. Of course, a rejection of what I say may strongly suggest that it is grounded in nothing more than a psychological quirk. Yet the reason that we are ever suspicious of incidental associations is precisely because we are seeking more worthwhile judgements on which we can agree, and for which we can acknowledge a genuine justification. The credentials of my judgement will be that it expresses something deliberate and considered about the way I attend to the work. And an agreement in my descriptions suggests an agreement in how we all approach the piece of music – a kind of congruence in the way we attend to it. If there is indeed a stony aspect to the Haydn slow movement, as I have suggested, then my experience of it is a function of the particular kind of attention that I have brought to bear on it. But I will have learned to do this, and so will many other listeners.

So the philosophical interest in our experience of music under a given aspect lies in the nature of our attention to the music, largely governed by our own volition. Roger Scruton has expressed the point well:

> Reference to a 'response' or an 'experience' seems entirely inappropriate simply because it seems to ignore the evident intellectual content of the judgement. What is interesting about an aesthetic experience is ... not the experience in its entirety but rather the thought that lies at its heart.[7]

But there remains a problem. For it is clear that there is a world of difference between entertaining an aspect in a piece of music – that is, entertaining a judgement which one believes must be an adequate move in the game of criticism on the grounds of its progenitor's bona fides – and hearing the aspect for oneself. And it might then be objected on the strength of this that the crucial element in such an experience of the music remains mysterious. In what does the 'dawning' of an aspect consist? Before tackling this objection, powerful as it as first appears, we should notice what it cannot achieve. Under no circumstances could this strange enlightenment *constitute* the grounds of our understanding judgements concerning a certain aspect. The realisation of a particular aspect is possible only for someone who is sufficiently prepared to accommodate its force, adequacy and applicability when he really hears it for the first time in the notes themselves.

Again it will be objected that in using the phrase 'really hearing for the first time' I am grounding the relevant judgement in an experience (clearly the reverse of my general enterprise). And indeed there is a clear temptation to regard the 'dawning' of an aspect as either the central component of our experience of a particular passage, or even as the experience in its entirety. This is simply a mistake, and one which seems to rest on a failure clearly to distinguish the content of an experience from its form. Wittgenstein was clear enough on this score, showing how the 'special feeling' we may get from a given passage – heard, for instance, as a conclusion being drawn – is identifiable only by reference to the notes themselves, and as such has a cognitive basis. It is not some extra, independent sensation that somehow validates what we had previously only believed. Nor is it the criterion that we understand the musical passage (see, for example, *Zettel* para. 165). Nevertheless, there is a clear difference between merely entertaining that a passage is to be heard as a conclusion, and hearing it as such oneself. The question therefore is, In what does this difference consist?

Peter Lewis, in his interesting and acute article 'Wittgenstein on words and music' puts it like this:

> In understanding the nature of this experience of music, it is important to understand that there are not, as it were, two things going on in my soul ... hearing the music and applying the concept, such as 'conclusion'. For there is a difference between hearing that this is a conclusion and hearing this as a conclusion.[8]

But the answer that he suggests is, in my view, both mistaken and unnecessary: 'To hear the music as a conclusion is to make the concept "conclusion" part of your experience of the music, to hear the music through the concept or through the meaning of the word conclusion.'[9] This is not at all clear; in particular to regard the concept 'conclusion' as a part of the experience seems directly at odds with regarding the concept as that through which the music is heard, and therefore as part of the form of the experience. This latter way of putting it seems much more natural. But in any case Lewis has himself given an answer, earlier on the same page, which to my mind is more complete and true: 'There is a change in the way I hear or experience this bit of music which is at the same time a development in my understanding of it. If I could play the piano, I think I would play this differently.'[10]

And, in fact, this is precisely what we should expect from Lewis, since his approach, as well as his inflections, proceeds directly out of Wittgenstein. The cognitive change in my understanding may indeed give rise to a different or intensified feeling in connection with the passage, but the sensation is not the criterion of my understanding, for I could have the understanding without the sensation, but not the reverse.

Strangely, Scruton too appears at one point to be the victim of this assumption that the content of our experience can somehow embrace its mode, although he conveys this error in a characteristically mysterious passage which begins with a sound enough dictum:

> In aesthetic appreciation we might say that the perception of an object is brought into relation with a thought of the object ... the object serves as a focal point on which many thoughts and feelings are brought to bear ... the thoughts and feelings that are aroused by art can, nonetheless, become part of our experience of it. They enter as an inalienable element into the experience itself, and transform it without diverting it from its original object.[11]

Again, the most surprising thing about this incredible passage is that it is so totally unnecessary. If our perception of an art-object is, plausibly, brought into relation with thoughts (and feelings) then this is because the object is considered through the mediation of those thoughts and feelings. As Scruton himself notes, art directs rather than arouses feelings.[12] If he intends merely that the way we experience the art-object must stand in some relation to the object itself, then this is trivially true. If, on the other hand, he intends that the mode of the experience (the thought that underlies it) in some sense be a part of the content of the experience, then this need only be stated to reveal its internal contradiction.

It is we who supply, in our imagination, those aspects that the work in some unclear sense 'calls up' in us, as Scruton expends considerable energy to demonstrate. However naturally a given aspect may appear to arise, this can happen only for those who are attending to the object in the right kind of way – those who have been inducted into this way of looking at things, into this particular game of judgement. And thus the burden of responsibility for the reading of an aspect – and hence for seeing it at all – rests on the way in which we attend to the object: namely the mode of our experience, or the thought that is brought into relation with the perception, as Scruton would put it. After all, as he says, the interesting thing about aesthetic experience is the thought that lies at its heart.

Let us take the example of hearing a passage as a conclusion – the example that appears to preoccupy Lewis. We might say that, as Lewis suggests, in hearing a passage as a conclusion, part of what we experience is the concept 'conclusion', and as such the concept becomes part of the content of our experience, alongside the auditory perception. The alternative must be that the concept 'conclusion' is somehow adjectival on the experience – directs the form of the experience. In other words, the concept must either be part of the experience which is *had* or it must be part of the *having*. Scruton's own more general account commits him to the latter view, which is precisely what we would expect. Scruton's own examination of aspects leads him to a number of claims concerning them: they are subject to the will of the perceiver, they are a cognitive product, they are divorced from any belief as to their actual inherence in the objects that sustain them, and they may be sustained by the very objects which other views simultaneously hold to display contrary aspects. All of these considerations underline the point that the perceiving of aspects consists in a certain kind of attention that we direct towards an object or an event. For example, we learn to regard certain kinds of musical events – cadences for instance – as conventional forms of 'conclusion', and we bring this idea to bear on the musical passage by our own volition. But we may be subsequently persuaded to adopt a more detailed or a more extended view of the same text, in the light of which we could abandon or revise our hearing of the same passage as a conclusion. Perhaps, after all, there is something to be said for regarding it as merely an intake of breath before some larger pronouncement – and so on. And with practice we learn automatically to assign certain descriptions to certain kinds of passages, almost as part of the data of the works which we hear and bring under our particular cognitive tendencies in our listening. It seems, then, that this 'thought which lies at the heart' of our aesthetic experience of listening to music is after all the cognitive form which our experience takes. And then it becomes misleading and irrelevant to attempt to assimilate this thought into the experience itself.

And so when an aspect 'dawns' for us – when we are able to say,

'Yes, now I see how it's to be played' – what has changed is the mode of our attention. We do not avail ourselves of some new or intensified sensation, but rather we make new or intensified judgements; we connect where previously we had failed to connect, and so on. We hear what we had failed to hear, and I think that this is what Lewis describes as 'a development in my understanding'. The criterion that we have grasped a new, altered or refreshed aspect is not the sensation that accompanies our understanding, but the understanding itself – the judgements that we are now able to make. To say that the musical passage now means something for me, where previously it did not, is simply to say that I can now grasp and arrange important aspects of the music in my understanding, by virtue of my own judgements rather than the judgements of somebody else.

An example from my own experience involves a quite highly differentiated aspect, namely the dramatic power of the 'return' in a sonata-form movement. (It is interesting, though easily overlooked, that all structures are aspects of their constituent notes.) The movement in question is the opening movement of Sibelius's Third Symphony. I had listened to this movement many times in the light of a summary grasp of the mechanics of sonata form, and so I must to an extent have been preparing myself for an eventual realisation of the drama of the structure. I must have been accruing the kinds of expectations that can be uniquely fulfilled by sonata form. And one day I must have become ready for this fulfilment. The climax of the development section, in which glimpses of the opening material pile on top of one another over a pedal leading-note, bursts into an exultant restatement of the opening in a purified form (having passed the *aqua regia* test of the development). On this one occasion, as I distinctly remember now, some twelve years later, my apprehension of these processes became instead a realisation of great intensity. To borrow Scruton's memorable phrase, the music 'came alive in the notes themselves'. But the additional feature of *this* experience was not some mystical, inner sensation but rather the realisation of the fulfilment of judgements that I had already learned to handle. Only when my expectations were sufficiently formed and differentiated could they be satisfied in quite this unique way. So the interesting thing about this experience – undoubtedly an aesthetic one – remains its intellectual character. Ideas which I simply acquired and used in a speculative and groping way became, over time, more properly

aligned and directed – my listening became more considered,
informed and specialised. The sonata structure became no longer
the object of my listening, but the *mode*. Now I listened in the light
of what I knew and not in its shadow.

The critical extracts with which we began this discussion
flourished through the metaphors which they employed as the
principal advocates of their respective positions. In each case the
reading was expressed through the metaphor. It remains, then, for
us to discuss this special kind of description – if indeed a metaphor
be a description at all. For it is clear that in one sense, the
expressions 'beads on a string' or 'crystal surface' are, in the special
contexts in which they occur, not giving us information as we
ordinarily understand it, at all.

The chief role of the metaphors in the critical passages was as the
focus of persuasive commendation of the readings each expressed.
So perhaps we should begin a discussion of metaphor here by
asking, not 'How do they work?', but 'What are they for?'. It is my
claim that a part of the essence of a judgement employing
metaphor is that it be essentially persuasive. And this is immediately distinct from the simple game of giving information. As
Wittgenstein points out in *Culture and Value*:

> I give someone an explanation, and tell him 'It's as though . . .',
> then he says, 'Yes, now I understand it', or, 'Yes, now I see how
> it's to be played'. It's most important that he didn't *have* to accept
> the explanation; it's not as though I had, as it were, given him
> conclusive reasons.[13]

But, of course, the speaker must be telling us about the music as
well as about himself. Cardus's remark about Horowitz's performances of Scarlatti is not merely a report about his own nervous
system. He wants us to hear the music the way that he hears it, and
this must be a practical possibility if his remark is to be regarded as
intelligible; furthermore, it must be the case that we could come to
hear the music like that partly through the agency of the metaphor.

Legion are the writers who have claimed that when an expression is used metaphorically it undergoes a shift in meaning. They
are all wrong, Max Black foremost (and most dazzlingly) among
them.[14] As William Charlton has shown, a metaphor retains its
normal meaning from its primary appearance as a straightforward
description. It is precisely because the metaphor has no straightfor-

ward application in its metaphorical appearance that it achieves what it does – the fruitful collision in our imagination of semantically irreconcilable ideas.[15] The intelligibility of the metaphor is therefore only a function of its meaning as a straightforward description – it can neither be identified with, *nor divorced from* that meaning.

It may be thought that I am assigning use to meaning, and not, more properly, the reverse, and hence conflating meaning and use. But we are obliged to distinguish between the meaning of the expression, which must be its normal or primary one (or as Charlton would put it, the semantically 'permitted' meaning) and the intelligibility of an expression whose use is obviously not semantically permitted on the kind of occasion we are discussing. It is not a part of the meaning of 'crystal', not even an extended part, that it should denote a feature of a musical structure; and it is only an extended part of the meaning of 'surface' that it should be applied to music in this way. And the power of the image of the 'crystal surface' arises directly out of this dislocation of meaning. It is the collision of ideas that gives insight, if the metaphor is a successful one. Indeed, I have claimed that this particular image is eminently successful, but I can appeal to no logical grounds in support of my claim. For the remark gives me no information of any kind that I could conclusively verify.

What, then, does the metaphor achieve? As Charlton puts it

> We do best to define metaphorical use in terms of ends, saying that the end for which words are transferred from their proper sphere of application must be in some way aesthetic . . . a living metaphor is an expression used in a way which the user knows to be inapplicable, for the purpose of securing an aesthetic advantage.[16]

And here at least, Black agrees that an account of the operation of metaphor may more fruitfully be sought in its purpose than in a discussion of its meaning, extended, altered or otherwise: 'There is . . . a sense of "metaphor" that belongs to "pragmatics" rather than to "semantics" – and this sense may be the one most deserving of attention.'[17]

Most statements involving metaphors are simply false. It is just because they are false, and patently, unabashedly so, that we are alerted to a different kind of understanding of them. The example that Black discusses is 'Man is a wolf'. The expression means no more and no less than that Man is a wolf, and the statement is literally false (although the corresponding simile, namely 'Man is like a wolf' is true for certain respects of men and wolves). And therefore the point of saying that Man is a wolf is something different from the point of making an empirical statement. Donald Davidson's excellent discussion of metaphor examines what this point could be.

> Metaphors cannot be paraphrased, but I think that this is not because metaphors say something too novel for literal paraphrase, but because there is nothing there to paraphrase ... a metaphor doesn't say anything beyond its literal meaning (nor does its maker, in using the metaphor, say anything beyond the literal). This is not, of course, to deny that a metaphor has a point, nor that the point can be brought out by using further words. ... [18]
>
> ... to suppose [metaphor] can be effective only by conveying a coded message is like thinking a joke or a dream makes a statement which a clever interpreter can restate in plain prose. Joke or dream or metaphor can, like a picture or a bump on the head, make us appreciate some fact – but not by standing for or expressing that fact. ... How many facts or propositions are conveyed by a photograph? None, an infinity, or one great unstateable fact? Bad question. A picture is not worth a thousand words, or any other number. Words are the wrong currency to exchange for a picture. [19]

Metaphors call our attention to some aspect of the situation, object or event at which they are aimed – or, better, they direct our attention in ways that we had not foreseen and could not, perhaps, describe through literal judgements. As such, they are perhaps not merely devices for securing what Charlton calls 'aesthetic advantage', but actually aesthetic events themselves. And in trying to grasp and obey the challenge of a metaphor we elucidate the metaphor through the development in our understanding of, say, the piece of music at which it is aimed.

If metaphors do not say things in the literal sense (beyond the literal meaning of the words, which produces falsity) then we are not required to believe a metaphorical judgement in order to share it. Belief and disbelief are not at home here. Interestingly, as

Scruton points out at some length, the same is true of aspects. We don't believe or disbelieve in the inherence of an aspect in a figure in the process of seeing it there. Indeed if we believed that the aspect was 'really there' then we wouldn't have seen it as an aspect at all; we would not have stood at the right conceptual distance from the aspect – a point which is developed in detail by Howard Mounce.[20]

It also follows that the intelligibility of a metaphor is divorced from truth conditions. The grounds of our understanding of a metaphor lie, not in our ability to verify the judgement in which it appears, but in something else. I have already hinted at the solution. The grounds of intelligibility of the metaphor are at least partly determined by its ability to persuade us, or to persuade our neighbour, of the value and adequacy of a particular vision. At first sight, this seems naturally to fall into circularity. For it seems that to be persuaded by a metaphorical judgement we have first to understand it. To rebut this charge I am required to show that there are independent grounds for the appropriateness of a judgement other than our ability to follow it on a given occasion – and it is my claim that these grounds are to be found in the general technique or game of judgements that we share with the speaker who gives us the metaphor. It will be the task of succeeding chapters to bolster this claim.

There are certain other things that we can say at this stage about the operation of metaphors. Scruton has claimed that we can substitute what he calls 'acceptance conditions' for the more usual truth conditions which underpin judgements that say something in the straightforward descriptive sense. And he allocates this role to our experiences of the art-object being characterised by the metaphor. If we hear it in the way prescribed by the metaphor, then we'll accept the account. If we don't, we won't. The problem with this is that as we have seen, the experience is itself founded on judgement. It is our capacity to make certain kinds of judgement that frames our experience of the music. For example, it is essentially through our fluency in the system of judgements that describe sonata form that we come to hear a movement as a sonata structure; only thus can we experience the music in this way. However, Scruton's suggestion does lead to a promising refinement. It may well be that it is our capacity to make figurative judgements of certain recognisable kinds that will frame our ability to understand the figurative judgements of other people. In other words, this is another kind of language game, only a highly specialised and differentiated kind. The value of applying our imaginations in this non-linear, non-rational way may be a value that is central, fundamental, understood and shared within the fairly well-defined circle of people who involve themselves with aesthetic objects. Such people will have learned to expect and to face up to judgements of a totally non-literal kind – and they will have prepared themselves to look past the meaning of the words to the non-literal reason or point behind their use.

There is a further respect in which the account of metaphor directs our enquiry towards judgement, and away from undifferentiated experience, and here too there is an interesting parallel with Scruton's account of aspect perception. He suggests that it makes sense to urge or instruct someone to perceive an aspect ('Hear it like *this* . . .') and that perceiving aspects is by this token subject not to our beliefs, but to our volition. And we have suggested that it is natural to think of metaphorical judgements in terms of the advocacy or persuasion or even instruction towards a particular reading. Metaphors, if striking and successful, are self-commending. It makes sense to suppose that we can be, as it were, instructed to hear a passage of music under this or that description, even though a literal application of the description would produce falsity. It makes sense to be instructed to attend to the music in this or in that way. And so it becomes natural to construe a powerful metaphor in terms of giving just such an instruction.

Obviously there are risks in such an account. For instance we should not suppose that in giving someone an instruction of this sort we are somehow giving them a complete programme or recipe for listening. As Wittgenstein has pointed out[21] the expressiveness of an aesthetic object or situation '*consists* to some degree in incalculability' and I think this must be true of our metaphors as well. It is a commonplace in philosophy that metaphors may degenerate into straightforward descriptions through acquiring an established use that can be given truth conditions – the genuine metaphor turns into a description with an extended meaning, such that a judgement that would once have been false, but worthwhile, becomes true (in an extended sense of the meaning of the expression) but pointless or uninteresting. Indeed to talk about 'programmes' for listening at all invites parallels with avowedly 'programmatic' music where the items in the musical text are assigned to depict certain scenes or events and thus acquire a kind of codified set of signs. One of the reasons why the more adventurous and accomplished listener will tend to avoid this sort of reading of music is that, in addition to a dislike of an extra-musical 'crutch' (*pace* Langer[22]) the strict assignation of an expressive phrase to a real-life 'counterpart' destroys the expressive relation itself, replacing it with a descriptive one. The music may stand for something as its lieutenant, but under these circumstances it can hardly express it in the aesthetic sense.

Lastly, I think it is worth looking at the way that metaphors directed at art-objects (or at anything else for that matter) are like art-objects themselves. It is for this reason that I referred to the figurative side of the critic's vocabulary as the vocabulary of the poet. For when we succeed in conveying an insight via a fruitful metaphor, what we have done is not merely to reflect on the aesthetic object but to engage in it. The critic is, as Davidson wryly puts it, in 'benign competition' with the author or the poet or the composer.[23]

Wittgenstein draws our attention to the distinctively aesthetic functions of speech in the *Philosophical Investigations* (where he spends so much time comparing recognised aesthetic situations with the way words mean or have meaning):

> We speak of understanding a sentence in the sense in which it can be replaced by another which says the same, but also in the sense in which it cannot be replaced by any other (any more than one musical theme can be replaced by another).[24]

This is the sense that is so important in our critical judgements. And this is precisely what we should expect, for inasmuch as the artist operates through the medium of tone, rhythm, colour and form, metre and rhyme, implication and metaphor, so too we must understand, if at all, through the same means. And so our judgements must reflect this and be informed and imbued and structured through this same 'incalculability'.

I have tried to illuminate critical language by showing it to be the equipment of a technique, a set of judgements, and a shared and participatory game. But what secures the *meaning* of the terms in this language? Are there rules to the game? And can just anybody play? It is to these questions that we must now turn.

Notes

1. Ludwig Wittgenstein, *Lectures and Conversations on Aesthetics, Psychology and Religious Belief* (Basil Blackwell, 1966), p. 4.
2. Wilfred Mellers, *Bach and the Dance of God* (Faber & Faber, 1980), pp. 55–6.
3. Alan Walker (ed.), *Robert Schumann: The Man and his Music* (Barrie & Jenkins, 1972), p. 101.
4. Neville Cardus, Notes to Columbia recording of Horowitz (MQ 499, 1962), p. 11.
5. Ludwig Wittgenstein, *Culture and Value* (Basil Blackwell, 1980), pp. 51e–2e.
6. Susanne Langer, *Philosophy in a New Key* (Harvard University Press, 1951), Ch. VIII.
7. Roger Scruton, *Art and Imagination* (Methuen, 1974), p. 78.
8. Peter Lewis, 'Wittgenstein on words and music', *Br. J. Aesthetics*, Vol. 17, 1977, 118.
9. Ibid.
10. Ibid.
11. Scruton, *Art and Imagination*, p. 155.
12. Ibid., p. 77.
13. Wittgenstein, *Culture and Value*, p. 69e.
14. Max Black, 'Metaphor', *Proceedings of the Aristotelian Society*, (1954/5).
15. William Charlton, 'Living and dead metaphors', *Br. J. Aesthetics*, Vol. 15, 1975, 172–8.
16. Ibid., pp. 177–8.
17. Black, 'Metaphor', pp. 2–8.
18. Donald Davidson, 'What metaphors mean', *Critical Enquiry*, Autumn (1978), p. 32.
19. Ibid., p. 46.
20. H. O. Mounce, 'Art and real life', *Philosophy*, April 1980.
21. Wittgenstein, *Culture and Value*, p. 73e.
22. Langer, *Philosophy in a New Key*, pp. 242–3.
23. Davidson, 'What metaphors mean', p. 47.
24. Ludwig Wittgenstein, *Philosophical Investigations* (Basil Blackwell, 1967), para. 531.

4
Expression and Gesture

We have distinguished judgements involving metaphors – such as the judgements about the 'crystal surface' of Scarlatti's piano music – from judgements which use descriptions like 'cadence', 'fugal opening' and 'tritone'. In the latter case we know the conditions for the truth of such judgements. But in the case of metaphors we do not know them: indeed we do not know how to make sense of the idea that they might be 'true' or 'false' at all – truth and falsity do not feature in this sort of talk at all. It looks as though that feature of a judgement which makes it expressive, cannot be examined and understood as if it were a description.

We must now ask what it is for us to understand such judgements, and we must try to account for this 'context of persuasion'. For no judgement can have sense which is not in principle open to the understanding of other people. So the nature of this understanding is crucial to our enquiry. If we cannot establish it, or if we cannot subsequently describe it, then we cannot seriously sustain our account of aesthetic judgement as it now stands.

This is a rather daunting task. For we are not merely saying that as it happens it is not usually helpful to look for the proof of a given aesthetic judgement, or to look for the demonstration of the correctness of a metaphor. We are saying that it does not make sense to ask this. It is part of what we mean by an aesthetic judgement or a metaphor that they cannot be proved or demonstrated in this way. Correctness and proof hold no place in this kind of discourse. And yet it would appear that without an agreed meaning to the characterisations which we use in our judgements, they become pointless or even incoherent. They could mean all things to all men – and this is just another way of saying they would mean nothing to anybody. So we seem forced to allow that the meaning of the constituents in an aesthetic judgement be in some sense secure, and understood to be secure. In other words, it seems there must be some agreement as to what the expressions used in an aesthetic judgement actually mean. But in view of what we have said about such judgements being grounded in a context of persuasion rather than of demonstration, we are forced to conclude that the basis of agreement as to the meaning of aesthetic judgements and their metaphors such as the 'physicality' of a Bach fugue is somehow different from the basis of agreement as to the meaning of descriptions such as that a particular passage involves a repeated right hand arpeggio over an ostinato bass.

One possibility is that the distinction is not as startling as it might at first appear. For whether or not language as a whole is learned ostensively (and there are strong, perhaps overwhelming arguments to suppose that it is not) people's grasp of it can, once current, be confirmed ostensively. Criteria for the correct application of a particular description can be detailed and listed. They can then be brought to bear on any given occasion. This is the bedrock of that agreement in meaning on which the coherence of language depends. Now it might be possible to show that, for someone who is practised or conversant with a particular approach to aesthetic judgement, he will be using a form of critical language which has specifiable aspects, meanings which command the automatic agreement of others who use this same critical approach, and which can be appealed or pointed to as criteria for the applicability of a certain judgement to a certain aesthetic situation. But the moment we try to think of examples of judgements that would satisfy this account, we find that they are almost exclusively technical, such as descriptions of rules of harmony and counterpoint. Or if they involve images at all, they are precisely those stale and predictable images that have the least interest, either for the conscientious listener, or for the philosopher engaged in an account of critical language. These are precisely those expressions which do, in fact, have secondary truth grounds for their meaning and for their use. If there is a basis of agreement in the meanings of metaphors and aesthetic expressions, it cannot be secured by so direct a route.

Another possibility is that whilst we could not look for criteria of the *correct* application of a certain expression, we might be able to look for criteria of its *appropriateness*. While no aesthetic judgement can of course be logically compelling in the sense that certain empirical descriptions follow from certain others, perhaps we can give a systematic account of why some expressions are persistently preferable to some others, in any given context. And maybe an agreement of this rather *ad hoc* kind would be enough to secure the meaning of the expressions concerned. The only trouble with this is that criteria are not, of course, *ad hoc* at all, except on the very high level of generality at which whole families of description could ultimately be traced back to behaviour of a very general sort. Ultimately there is, perhaps, a sense in which the existence of aesthetic discourse at all is wedded to a certain kind of collective behaviour. But this level of 'agreement' is at the foundation of the meaning of aesthetic discourse, and fundamentally to be distinguished from local, context-related agreements in particular usage. Within an established discourse, criteria for individual preference cannot be produced as it were by local agreement. This is not what we mean by a criterion. A criterion does not give simple support to preferences or inclinations to choose this description rather than that. A criterion provides us with the calculability, the logical compulsion that says if such-and-such a description is correct, then, from the meanings of the terms involved, so many others will be also. It is this calculability that is alien to the spirit and enterprise of metaphorical expressions; in short, alien to their point, and, as such, alien to their meaning. For we have stressed that aesthetic judgements which involve metaphors are always literally false – that is, systematically and recursively false by the application of any criteria whatsoever. Therefore if they have meaning, it is a kind of meaning that is secured *despite*, rather than through, criteria.

A third possibility then is that all talk of criteria is out of place here. But this seems to leave the burden of explaining the security of meaning of aesthetic expressions unsupported, except by an appeal to some form of agreement which we have yet to describe. It looks as though such agreement would have to be tied superficially to the persuasive force which a particular judgement carries with it. And on first examination this link appears to be circular. Yet of the possibilities open to us this seems the most promising. And I hope to show in this chapter that Wittgenstein uses this line of reasoning in his forays into aesthetics. I hope we can develop what Wittgenstein says into a respectable and more complete account of our understanding of meaning in the absence of criteria.

Indeed, Roger Scruton seems to have taken his cue from Wittgenstein when he engages in an elaborate discussion of truth conditions and of what he calls 'non-descriptive meaning' in his *Art and Imagination*.[1] How consciously he intends to tie the meaning of aesthetic judgements to their illocutionary force (in this case, persuasive value) is not clear, since at least a part of his overt

enterprise is to show how aesthetic experiences can be characterised independently of their actually being 'had', whereas the
persuasive value of an aesthetic judgement seems to be tied in
some degree to its role in bringing about an aesthetic experience of
some kind in the hearer. For Scruton insists that the meaning of
aesthetic judgements is secured essentially by what he calls
'acceptance conditions' being fulifled on the part of the hearer.
And these acceptance conditions turn out to be none other than
aesthetic experiences themselves. Before we examine this seeming
paradox (which looks very like that afflicting the third of the
possibilities I listed above) it is instructive to follow Scruton's
reasoning more closely.

He usefully distinguishes between the formal security of meaning and the 'epistemological' security of meaning, of these troublesome expressions (Scruton refers to them as 'aesthetic descriptions', though I prefer to avoid this label). And in this way he tries
to show how we can bypass the formal requirement that the
meaning of a sentence be given by the conditions for its truth.
Scruton begins by claiming that the semantic theory of meaning (a
formal theory) and the speech-act theory of meaning (an epistemological theory) are answers to two different questions. The semantic theory offers a recursive answer to the question, 'What meaning
does any given sentence have?', whereas the speech-act theory
aims to answer the question 'What is it for a sentence to have
meaning?'. This latter question is highly general, and as Scruton
points out, it is easier for answers to a question of this type to cover
obstructive cases such as sentences involving metaphors than it is
for a recursive answer concerning individual sentences, which
must run up against a specific analysis of the offending sentence.
Yet Scruton finds that this difficulty can be met by limiting the
scope of the semantic theory, which he claims does not tackle the
meanings of individual predicates. Central to this move is his view
of the truth condition account of meaning. In his introduction, he
lays out the unargued assumptions that will underlie his argument, and among these is the assumption that 'the interesting
features of a term . . . are the features which govern the truth and
falsehood of a sentence where the term occurs'.[2] Furthermore,

> There is a central category of sentences, including many present
> tense singular declarative sentences, that are essentially tied to
> truth conditions, in that no account can be given of the meaning

of one of these sentences, that does not refer to the conditions for its truth. . . . And giving sense to sentences of this class is a condition of giving sense to any sentences whatsoever.[3]

Many aesthetic judgements are made in sentences that are formally of a present tense declarative type, for example 'op. 120 is . . . a quite fantastic assembly of reflections rayed off from a vibrating centre'[4] as are many interjections of a more generally illuminating kind – compare Samuel Butler's reference to the chord of the diminished seventh as the 'Clapham Junction' of music. Although these sentences lack truth conditions in the strong sense of 'the observable states of affairs that make sentences true'[5] Scruton holds that the fault lies in the analysis of the individual predicates concerned, and a semantic theory is silent about these. 'Provided these predicates (such as the "good" of ethics) have the normal syntactical properties, then they will present no obstacle to semantic theory. . . .'[6] Interestingly, the comparison with the 'good' of ethics suggests that Scruton is assimilating aesthetic judgements to judgements of value, and while there may be important objections to such an assimilation, his motive seems consistent with the idea that aesthetic judgements have a persuasive function.

It is worth recalling how many declarative sentences in aesthetic discourse have acquired truth conditions (for instance, stale metaphors) and these are directly explicable by a semantic theory. But for genuine metaphors, the most that Scruton has so far achieved is to show that semantic theory is non-commital about their meaning. It remains for him to show that an account of their meaning is possible.

To do this he relies heavily on the alternative speech-act theory of meaning, which he has been careful to deny has any conflict with semantic theory.

Because moral and aesthetic judgements have an indicative and assertoric form, they can be incorporated into a semantic theory along with all other indicative sentences. But once they have been fitted into the language in this way, it is inevitable that they should borrow the logical transformations of description . . . the real question is not how it is possible for such judgements to fit into the language as quasi-descriptions, but rather what is the point of their doing so.[7]

And it is here that he runs into the paradox concerning the possibility of independently describing aesthetic experiences. Aesthetic judgements, he maintains, can be examined for their meaning in terms of the intention behind their utterance (following Grice[8]); the intention behind a metaphorical utterance is to get someone to see the point of what you are saying, as in Neville Cardus's casual remark that Horowitz had the genius 'to ravish the piano and yet leave it chaste'.[9] Scruton tries to rescue this from the triviality into which it seems naturally to fall, by an appeal to the acceptance conditions for a given sentence. In other words, he at once sees the difficulty, which we noted above, in attempting to root the meaning of a judgement in its persuasive power. And his response is to expand the analysis of what it is to be persuaded by such a judgement, in an attempt to give an account of its meaning independently of the experience which the judgement is expressing. And in this I do not believe he is successful.

The problem could be summarised like this: a speech-act account would identify the meaning of an aesthetic judgement by referring to the intention behind its utterance. This intention would be, presumably, to commend the aesthetic experience which the judgement expresses. If, for example, I am struck by a literal stoniness or flinty quality in Janacek's Glagolitic Mass, then my intention in telling you this is at least partly to commend that way of listening to you. But immediately we see that the only way of differentiating the experiences which underlie aesthetic judgements is via the sentences which make up the judgements themselves. So it becomes futile to look for the identity of the meaning of the judgement in the intention which lies behind it. That intention is itself a matter for identification by means of the sentences concerned. The argument is circular. What is needed is some further ground of the identity, both of the sentence and of the intention behind its utterance.

Scruton looks for this ground in an account of the circumstances under which we accept an aesthetic judgement. And he distinguishes the conditions of acceptance of a judgement from states of affairs which might make it true. In this, I take him to be regarding truth grounds as merely one sort of condition of acceptance of a judgement, albeit the primary ground of acceptance of a primary or central class of judgements. His motives may be sound enough, but the example he offers as an illumination of this stage of his argument appears to be far too modest for his aim. He suggests an invented adjective, 'nuff', which we apply to something which attracts us and which consequently expresses an attitude rather than a belief.[10] As such it embodies a value which could be taught by extension from the part of our discourse concerned with feelings and tastes. Well, it would be most surprising if we could not in fact adapt and adopt terms in this way. But this is a very long way short of the highly differentiated expression of an aesthetic experience. 'Nuffness' is too readily assimilable to other simple equivalents – it is, effectively, translatable. But of course this is precisely the feature that is denied to aesthetic characterisations and to metaphors. Their value lies in their particularity, their unique adequacy to the experiences they express. When Keats describes the man who attains the shrine of Melancholy as one '... whose strenuous tongue / Can burst Joy's grape against his palate fine'[11] what he is saying cannot be translated into simpler sentences having truth conditions. Indeed Scruton's own later insistence, that it is our own experiences which validate for us the aesthetic judgements of others, must prove fatal to his account at this point. (See for instance his discussion of twelve tone music.[12]) For it looks as though those experiences are themselves differentiated only in terms of an understanding of the judgements in which they are expressed. And this seems to tie understanding a judgement to assenting to it; it makes agreeing with the judgement a logical condition of understanding it. One unattractive consequence of this is that it would not be possible significantly to deny an aesthetic judgement or any judgement involving a metaphor. For to deny something in any significant sense you have to understand it, and that seems to mean, for this kind of judgement, sharing it.

It is an important fact about any discourse that disagreement is possible; otherwise all utterances within it are equally valid, which is only another way of saying that none are. It is possible, however, that agreement or disagreement in a metaphorical judgement is grounded, as it were, in advance of the judgement, in a set of attitudes that are expressed in a *set* of judgements. Metaphors will tend to hold good within this viewpoint rather than within that; they will tend to express a particularity within this more general attitude rather than within that. As such, agreement in a metaphor may be a matter of the intensification of an attitude which is already shared, or not shared, by the hearer according to whether he accepts other sets of judgements which we could more easily examine. And indeed this seems the most likely way out of

Scruton's dilemma – a way out that has, I shall argue, been anticipated by Wittgenstein. A special consequence of there being no local criteria for the adequacy of a metaphor or of an expressive judgement is that the metaphorical or aesthetic judgement is apprehended only by one's in some sense coming to share it; the impact of such a judgement is what constituted its point. But this is explained in terms of the special place that such judgements hold within our more general critical vocabulary. Our expressive or metaphorical vocabulary has a general security of meaning that is given by its place within the wider critical vocabulary. It has been a part of our argument prior to this chapter that we make this highly specialised kind of judgement from the position of fluency in a certain lexicon of critical judgements. We learn to move through hackneyed images to genuinely fresh ones; but this applies to our understanding of the images given by others, equally and co-extensively with our ability to give such images ourselves. And I think that it is in this enlarged sense that Scruton's 'acceptance conditions' might prove fruitful.

Recall what we said about the 'dawning' of an aspect. What changes in our experience is the mode of attention – the way in which we attend to the aesthetic object. For example, my realisation of the drama of the sonata form, in the opening movement of Sibelius's Third Symphony, rested on the fulfilment or actualisation of judgements that I had already learned to respect and in some restricted sense to deploy on the right sort of occasion, but which I had not yet infused into what I heard in the required way. So this realisation was indeed what Peter Lewis called a 'development in my understanding'. It seems to me that two important things emerge from this. First, the development of my experience is internally related with the development of the judgements in which those experiences are expressed. Any account of the broadening of my experience is, in fact, an account of the development of my understanding, and this must be at least partly a verbal development. My experiences and the judgements which differentiate them are mutually dependent. One is not a criterion of the other: and to look for a criterion here is a mistake. When Scruton identified experiences as the acceptance condition for judgements we complained of the circularity arising from the requirement that those experiences be differentiated by judgements. Putting one before the other is an artificial division that cannot ultimately be sustained. A better way of viewing this is to regard our critical vocabulary as consisting co-extensively of our judgements and our experiences; and the acceptance condition for a judgement then becomes the development of our understanding – which must involve experience – to accommodate this new way of listening or looking. Each fresh metaphor is the expression, the vehicle and the mode of a new thought.

The second important thing to arise here is that we learn to recognise and to appreciate this kind of development in the understanding of other listeners – and this will be shown in what they say. Indeed it is only in the context of the judgements of our fellows that we can fully develop our own thoughts at all. Critical dialogue and discourse is necessary, not merely for the success, but for the very coherence of our own insight. And thus part of what it is to understand someone else's aesthetic judgements and expressions is simply our confidence in the validity and application of their general lexicon of aesthetic judgement, which we will in large measure share (assuming a certain common cultural background) and which tells us how their thought has developed and is developing. What makes the expression 'lean Tuesday'[13] or the supposition that the Scherzo of Beethoven's Fifth begins as 'a goblin walking quietly over the universe, from end to end'[14] intelligible, is not some isolated sensation or intuition on the part of the hearer, but his confidence in the other things that the speaker says, and the degree to which he shares the speaker's general vocabulary of judgement. If we know anything of what the speaker is inclined to say, we can know perfectly well when his installation of goblins into the scherzo is perverse, and when it is serious. We can know when it is simply about his nervous system, and when it really is directed at the music.

I have claimed that Wittgenstein's remarks on aesthetics give us a philosophically respectable account of the process of understanding here. He anticipates the central difficulty in Scruton's identification of acceptance conditions with 'experience' in the opening of the first *Lecture on Aesthetics*, where he examines the experience of aesthetic satisfaction and recognition, and then disposes of the seductive notion that some undifferentiated signal of satisfaction – he calls it a 'clicking' – could be the guarantor of the adequacy of even the intelligibility of a particular judgement. 'It is as though you needed some criterion, namely the clicking, to know the right thing has happened.'[15] No doubt it is a convenient label to say of the most satisfying expression that it 'clicks', but Wittgenstein denies that any useful inner phenomenon underlies this. It does not consist in something additional to the selection of our particular judgement or expression as being satisfying. The psychological predictability – in the causal sense – is Wittgenstein's main stalking horse here:

> You might say that the clicking is that I'm satisfied. Take a pointer moving into place opposite another one. You are satisfied *when* the two pointers are opposite one another. And you could have said this in advance. We are again and again using this simile of something clicking or fitting, when really there is nothing that clicks or fits anything.[16]

To identify the acceptance conditions of an aesthetic judgement with some experience – some clicking – which validates it is to risk invoking precisely this kind of undirected inner twinge. It risks putting the burden of explanation onto something that is itself undifferentiated, and epistemologically no more respectable than a sensation – exactly parallel to the emotivist mistake which we examined in Chapter 2 – rather than onto the proper support of a development in our understanding. (In fairness to Scruton, I do not think that he would be happy with any account that ran such a risk, and the way he expresses his account of acceptance conditions seems to me to be at odds with the better parts of his reasoning.)

Wittgenstein in fact supplies us with models for the basis of the kind of account we want. But before we examine those models, we have to acknowledge that some commentators have found difficulties in the *Lectures on Aesthetics*, and we have to ask whether they can be overcome, for if they cannot, then the basis of those models of understanding is in question. The affirmative answer, that the difficulties can be overcome, is provided in Roger Shiner's excellent article, 'Wittgenstein on the Beautiful, the Good and the Tremendous'. I shall briefly rehearse his reasoning. Shiner distinguishes two apparently conflicting themes in Wittgenstein's remarks – firstly a theme of the affective, and seemingly non-cognitive aspect to aesthetic response (as in, for example, Wittgenstein's case of the uneducated landlady[17]); and secondly an apparently rule-governed, and often dangerously paradigmatic view of aesthetic judgement (as in, for example, the proportions of the tailor's suit[18]). To these I would add a third – the uneasy fusion of the two main themes in the example concerning the 'discomfort' concerning the height of a door,[19] in that it is here that Wittgenstein seems to me to anticipate Shiner's vindication of him.

Well, does Wittgenstein adhere to a largely emotivist story where the 'chain of reasons' for an aesthetic choice or expression simply stops short at the personal inclinations of the speaker? Or does he indeed offer a systematic grouping of formal, checkable criteria for the validity of any given aesthetic judgement? To answer this, Shiner usefully locates the *Lectures* in the context of Wittgenstein's concurrently developing thought more generally, and by astute reference to the *Investigations* he draws out an interpretation of the nature of aesthetic 'reasons' which underpins the superficially affective terms such as 'beautiful', 'lovely' and so on, yet which at the same time releases the formal grip of the notion of 'correct' judgements. In this way he shows how we can free aesthetic judgement from the threat of crippling, paradigmatic certainty, such as would obtain in a genuinely truth-grounded context. It is the limits of the significant application of what Wittgenstein calls 'interjections' – such as, in this context, 'lovely', 'fine', etc. – which rescue those interjections from mere subjectivism. At the same time it is what Shiner calls the piecemeal or case-by-case assessment of each aesthetic expression which rescues these from the formal subjection to criteria for their 'correct' (sic) application.

In its way this synthesis is both elegant and acute. And we can extend it in our own terms: it is the lexicon or vocabulary of judgement-and-experience which we share with others that enables us to make imaginative incursions into the area of literal falsity – and metaphorical power – in our aesthetic judgements. We can assess each such incursion for its impact by referring to the bedrock of judgements which supports it, without at any stage invoking a criterion. Equally, when we confine ourselves to an 'interjection', it is our general vocabulary of judgement which underwrites what might otherwise be naive or undirected reaction. In this respect we can distinguish between the 'interjections' of a committed listener and the 'interjections' of a casual listener, someone perhaps like the landlady in Wittgenstein's example. It is the other things that they say which settle matters for us. So it is the context of vocabulary, in the sense in which I have been using the term, which gives sense and meaning to aesthetic expressions and interjections, a point that Wittgenstein illuminates by listing several possible such contexts, for example that of the Russian who admires an English sonnet but does not actually speak a word of English himself.[20]

Appended to the *Lectures on Aesthetics* is a lecture belonging to a course of *Lectures on Description*. In this lecture (for which we have only a single source, namely Rhees's notes) Wittgenstein rehearses both his aversion to causal or mechanical explanations of aesthetic choices, and the thinking behind the models of non-criterial judgement which we are shortly to examine. But it also contains a passage which perhaps exemplifies the worries that commentators have felt concerning the appearance of an emotivist account of choices:

> You may read a stanza. I let you all read it. Everyone reads it slightly differently. I get the definite impression that 'none of them has got hold of it'. Suppose then I read it out to you and say: 'Look this is how it ought to be'. Then four of you read this stanza, no one exactly like the other, but in such a way that I say: 'Each one is exactly certain of himself'. This is a phenomenon, being certain of yourself, reading it in *one way only*. He is absolutely exact as to what pause to make. I might say in this case that you four have got hold of it. I would have conveyed something to you. I would perfectly correctly say, that I have exactly conveyed to you the exact experience that I had.[21]

Superficially, it looks as though an inner certainty is the sole guarantor of the validity of the interpretation. Indeed it seems as though an air of conviction in those who read the stanza is what impresses Wittgenstein in this situation. But Shiner shows how we could, confronted by such an example, apply a case-by-case examination of what each of the readers is doing, through the agency of their backgrounds, their range of readings, the connections they are disposed to make. I would put it like this: we would have confidence in their conviction if we shared a vocabulary of judgements/experiences with them, as a background to this particular judgement or interpretation. From this point it is a matter of our coming to hear it in the same way they do – of developing our understanding in the same way that they have. It is always possible, of course, that someone may give an ill-considered reading which they would subsequently disavow. Or they may be

brought to withdraw it or to hold it less dogmatically. Alternatively, their interpretation may simply not touch us at all. Yet this
would not in itself undermine the value of the reading. It is
reduced to an emotivist or subjectivist level only if the necessary
context of judgement is missing. And this is something that we can
find out. Indeed, this is itself a part of what Shiner calls 'case-by-
case' examination (for which he usefully draws an analogy with
legal and judicial examination). Furthermore, our confidence in
such an examination is a part of what Scruton called acceptance
conditions for the judgements of a given person.

Here Shiner ties in a difficult passage from the *Investigations* to
underscore the force of his reasoning:

> What one acquires here is not a technique; one learns correct
> judgement. There are also rules, but they do not form a system,
> and only experienced people can apply them right. Unlike
> calculating rules.[22]

Here the introduction of the idea of 'rules' no longer threatens to
tie the judgement to a criterion; for a criterion can be described in
terms of a system, which Wittgenstein is ruling out; and the
contrast with calculating rules seems to suggest an interpretation
of the 'correct' that is divorced from verification. Shiner is implying
that these 'correct' judgements are acquired piecemeal, after the
manner of a case-by-case examination such as the one he is
advocating. And indeed this seems as reasonable an interpretation
as any of a particularly pithy and intractable passage. Nonetheless,
'correct' is an unhappy term, and Wittgenstein regulates its meaning in the models he offers us for non-criterial understanding, to
which we now turn.

Although his overt enterprise throughout much of the *Lectures*
is to get rid of causal or mechanical explanations for aesthetic
choices, the models he uses to prosecute this aim are instructive
beyond it. He discusses our understanding of facial expressions, of
cartoons, of gestures, and of the 'look' of arbitrary lines as opposed
to purposive or scripted lines; and he also discusses the mechanical replication of a painting as an illumination of several of the other
models. Taken together, I believe that they provide an account of
how we understand the application of expressions that have no
criterial basis; what is more I think that they do so in a perfectly
simple and accessible way that does away with the mystique that

appears to attach itself to this question.

The first model, and perhaps the most extensive, is that of facial expressions, and our recognition and interpretation of them. Wittgenstein uses the analogy of 'making a face' in a variety of contexts, for example as an illumination of characterisations of music:

> Such words as 'pompous' and 'stately' could be expressed by faces. Doing this, our descriptions would be much more flexible and various than they are as expressed by adjectives. If I say of a piece of Schubert's that it is melancholy, that is like giving it a face.[23]

The analogy seems to do a lot of work here. Wittgenstein could be inviting vagueness in his talk of 'flexible' descriptions, but one could as easily claim that each of the many faces which could be characterised as 'pompous' would have a more precise look to it than the independent adjective, heard *in vacuo*. If this is so, then actual facial expressions might accompany our verbal judgements to good effect, even to the point of serving aesthetic purposes. However, the more interesting point is that it is this variety of human faces which can be subsumed under 'pompous' which shows just how highly differentiated and acute is our recognition of facial expressions. The versatility of the human face depends on a highly differentiated reading on the part of someone seeing a particular facial expression. And this differentiation suggests the power of the model of facial expression for an account of our understanding of aesthetic expressions. It is the high degree of differentiation displayed by expressive objects and events (including pieces of music, and responses to pieces of music) that makes criteria for many of our judgements so inaccessible; there can be no criterion for a uniquely adequate expression other than the expression itself – which is to say, no criterion at all. Furthermore, this differentiation is what compels us to use metaphors to characterise aesthetic objects and events, instead of descriptions which have an indefinite range of application according to criteria. If we can sketch the basis of our recognition of facial expression, perhaps we can do as much for our cognition of aesthetic objects and judgements.

What, then, is this basis? Leaving aside individual psychological explanations for given cases, our recognition must be based, it seems, either on the general application of criteria, or on a piecemeal assimilation of innumerable different cases, which we assemble into a kind of open-ended catalogue.

Criteria would have the advantage of immediately guaranteeing agreement in judgement among those who were busy characterising a particular facial expression (and this would underwrite the significance of such characterisations as they produced). However, we soon find that we are unable to say what those criteria might be, for any given facial expression, in that a certain orientation of one face may yield a contrary expression if transferred to another person's face. It is true that we could give very general criteria for happy and sad faces (upturned or downturned corners of the mouth, for instance) but these apply only to non-problematic descriptions – such as 'sad' and 'happy' – which are not often very enlightening. It is the differences between expressions which might collectively be regarded as happy or sad, which are important. It is the 'flexibility' and 'variety' within general expression types that interest Wittgenstein, and which more closely model the particularity of aesthetic expressions. And for these differences we cannot specify criteria. Wittgenstein makes this explicit later in the *Lectures*:

> I may draw you a face. Then at another time I draw another face. You say: 'That's not the same face' – but you can't say whether the eyes are closer together, or mouth longer . . . or anything of this sort. 'It looks different, somehow!'.[24]

Indeed, not only can we not give a criterion for a particular expression, but two people may make the same expression through very different dispositions of their faces, measured in purely physical terms. And this suggests that what we mean by 'the same' expression is not something that is given by referring to a paradigm of a particular expression. 'A person who imitates another's face doesn't do it before a mirror, but it is a fact that there is such a thing as saying: "The face is so and so".'[25] Indeed, if the basis of calling two facial expressions 'the same' were a system of measurement, it would become futile ever to speak of imitating the expressions of another; for the notion of 'the same' expression on two palpably different physiognomies would become recursively false, and therefore meaningless. Again, the notion of 'the same' facial expression on the same face at different times raises the same questions: 'We may say correctly "his face has the same expression now as previously" – even though measurements yielded different results on the two occasions.'[26]

It seems clear from this that the identification of a facial expression on any given occasion is a matter, not of analysis but of a synthetic grasping of some kind of *gestalt*. There are no usable and isolable components to which we could refer across different occasions of 'the same' expression. Hence we do not use isolable components as such in the compilation and description of a facial expression even on the single occasion. 'Tender expression in music. It isn't to be characterised in terms of degrees of loudness or tempo. Any more than a tender facial expression can be characterised in terms of the distribution of matter in space.'[27] So our recognition of facial expressions seems not to rest on criteria at all. It is something we learn to do by example, but not through paradigmatic examples. It is as instantaneous as it is subtle, and we show that we have recognised a particular expression by what we say and do in response. We build up a vocabulary of expression, and we assess – if that is not too clinical a term – each case of seeing an expression as it occurs. We relate each case to what we have seen before, but we have the capacity to read an expression that we have not previously seen, relating it to expressions that we would call 'the same' or comparable on very different sorts of faces. Indeed, the lack of criteria shows that 'the same' has a special meaning in this context, and Wittgenstein sets himself to examine this in another model.

Harold Osborne, reviewing the *Lectures*[28] complained that Wittgenstein had taken no account of the difference between incidental facial expressions and the dispositional look on a particular person's face. This is a surprising claim, because just such a distinction underlies the model of cartoon representation, given in full in the fourth Lecture:

I draw a few dashes with a pencil and paper, and then ask, 'Who is this?' and get the answer: 'It is Napoleon'. . . . I can easily distinguish between a few scratches, on the one hand, and a picture of a man properly drawn, on the other. No one would say: 'this is the same as that' in one sense. But, on the other hand we say, 'That's Napoleon'. On one peculiar balance we say, 'This is the same as that'. On one balance the audience easily distinguishes between the face of the actor and the face of Lloyd

George. All have learnt the use of '='. And suddenly they use it in a peculiar way. They say 'This is Lloyd George!', although in another sense there is no similarity. An equality which we could call the 'equality of expression'. We have learnt the use of 'the same'. Suddenly we automatically use 'the same' when there is not similarity of length, weight or anything of the sort.[29]

What we intend by 'the same' is nothing to do with isolable components. It has nothing to do with anything that could be repeatable in a rule-governed way. There are no criteria for our recognition of 'the same' in this sense. Wittgenstein's phrase 'the equality of expression' encapsulates both the problem and its solution.

So far we can apply the model of recognition of a particular expression to our recognition of expression in an art-object – a form of reading that we apply, case by case, drawing on our vocabulary of other examples of expressions, never physically duplicated. And the ability to distinguish different senses of 'the same', different kinds of comparison, the 'equality of expression' crucial among them, facilitates our fitting verbal expressions including metaphors to the aesthetic objects and events. It is this that enables us to match one kind of image with another, to see that on one level the diminished seventh cord and Clapham Junction are 'the same'; to match the expression of the C minor Scherzo with the image of a goblin walking quietly from one end of the Universe to the other. This peculiar kind of matching is a kind of cartoon.

Interestingly, we are not taught to regard a certain type of cartoon as a caricature of Napoleon. We do not have to be shown in each new case of a previously uncaricatured face, that this is the operation that is being performed. We have learned, through a large number of individual cases, when to be alerted to this strange kind of equivalence. We can project real faces into their cartoon representations and see how they are the same, and how different. Yet the real face is not a criterion nor a paradigm for the caricature. Napoleon is not the paradigm for cartoons of him (nor Lloyd George for his stage representative). A definitively amusing cartoon of Napoleon might be perhaps a paradigm for other cartoons, but then those other cartoons would stand in relation to the paradigm as instances or copies of it, not as cartoons of *it*. The relation between the cartoon and its subject actually works by trampling upon the idea of a paradigm. It is just because, in one sense of the equals sign, a caricature is so grotesquely unlike its subject that it is read as a cartoon. Like metaphors, cartoons are structurally, recursively 'false'. That is their point, and this is part of what we learn when we learn to read them.

Our metaphors give aesthetic objects a face, sometimes a caricatured face. We caricature, however, with the fullest and most constructive intention. We caricature the aesthetic object because we could not reproduce it, and that is not our purpose. We want to stand in a purposive and revealing relation to the aesthetic object, not simply to re-present it. So our judgements and our metaphors are understood in the same sort of way that cartoons are understood. We are not merely reflecting, but intervening – our judgements are an image in the literal as well as the figurative sense. The image might be a failure, but this is settled, not by appealing to criteria or to paradigms, but by whether, and how, the image fits into the framework of images and judgements that we have in common with other listeners and viewers. A cartoon can fail through being unrecognisable *or* through being over-literal, but without failing to meet any isolable criteria. In the same way our judgements can fail to locate or to illuminate their object, yet without missing any specifiable points of reference. We can fail through being perverse, or through being over-cautious, over-literal. In each case we fail to stand at a sufficiently useful, but still usable, distance from the aesthetic object. We know when a cartoon succeeds or fails in doing this, and we can know when a judgement and an image or metaphor succeeds or fails. And it is this ability, underpinned not by rules or a technique but by experience and a vocabulary of judgements and of images, which secures the meaning of the terms used in the expressive judgements themselves.

If a metaphor is a useful or valuable one, it has what Wittgenstein calls this 'equality of expression' with its object. It expresses something of what the object expresses, some aspect of what the object expresses (and here it is important that not intentionally expressive objects alone may have expressive power; under the right circumstances any object or event might stand to its surroundings or to its spectators in an expressive or an aesthetic relation. And one sign of this could be that someone characterised the object or event by the use of a metaphor). It is also important that our grasp of a metaphor fails if it is mediated for us. It is diminished by paraphrase. For the moment we begin to attempt a paraphrase, we are trying to distinguish isolable and independent components. And in so doing we lose sight of the overall face which the image makes. It is as though we tried to convey, say, the Churchill family face by a list of component features – each feature being in itself in need of further, and futile, analysis, a point wittily brought out by Bambrough.[30] And this is why we understand painting only through a conception of colour and line, or poetry through a conception of metre and assonance, or music through tone and rhythm – and in the same way, metaphor only through an active collision of the ideas that the metaphor fuses together. Only through a grasp of the mode of expression of an aesthetic object can we generate, or respond to, an image that can pull the same face, or 'draw' its expression as a 'cartoon' in words. A metaphor stands in 'equality of expression' to the aesthetic relation it portrays or illuminates. And only by grasping it in this unmediated way can we grasp its expressive power. We cannot separate the expressive power of a face, or of a minuet[31] from the face or the minuet itself. We cannot give substitute descriptions. We might, perhaps, be able to give a verbal image that pulled such a face, or drew such a caricature. But this image, this metaphor must itself be understood directly. A paraphrase is not equal in expression to the metaphor, because a paraphrase is not expressive at all.

It makes sense to ask someone to explain what he means by a particular image, but it also makes sense for him to refuse to do so, or to offer in explanation further images. Sooner or later we must grasp an image in an unmediated recognition of its face, its *gestalt*, or give up the attempt. If we do not see the face that one judgement makes, we can really gain access to it only through seeing a face 'equal to it in expression' made by another judgement. Indeed, this can be seen as a logical backstop that overcomes the futility of systematic explanation demanded by, for example, Langer's story about the similar logical forms of a verbal image and its object, or of a piece of music and its extra-musical programme. For we are always entitled to ask, of those who suppose that there is a relation between the logical forms of, say, parallel diatonic thirds and the hurrying of Mary, Joseph and the unborn Child to Bethlehem:[32] On what do you base your univocal ascription of a common feature in respect of which these two logical forms are similar? How are we to understand two categorically different predications of a single morphology? For this is to invoke a translation, a criterion-dependent analysis exactly where one cannot be sustained. The answer is in reality that this is not the place to analyse. The whole point about our understanding of 'equality of expression' is that it has nothing to do with criteria. Our entry into a particular expression is via an image that we *grasp*: and it is our general *experience* that puts us in a position to be able to do this, not logic. The rules do not form a system.

The futility of paraphrase comes out in Wittgenstein's next model. In the attached *Lecture on Descriptions*, he discusses the replication of a painting by a system of grid-references. In fact he introduces the example quite casually in the course of a discussion of mechanical descriptions of gestures.

> Suppose we said, that we cannot describe in words the express-ion of God in Michelangelo's 'Adam'. 'But this is only a matter of technique, because if we drew a lattice-work over his face, numbered, I could just write down numbers and you might say: "My God! It's grand!"' It wouldn't be any description. You wouldn't say such a thing at all. It would only be a description if you could paint (act?) according to this picture, which of course, is conceivable. But this would show that you can't at all transmit the impression by words, but you'd have again to paint.[33]

Furthermore, the procedure by which we 'painted again' would need scrutiny; if all we had done was to paint out according to grid numbers, it would not follow that we had painted a picture, even if by physical measurement our reproduction was indistinguishable from the original. Measurable mistakes would not in any case be the criterion for our having achieved the same expression in the copy as in the original. In so far as we grasped the original picture and its expression, then a grid system of replication would be foreign to our understanding. We would not apprehend the picture in those terms. Any copy we produced would be more likely to achieve 'the same' or 'equivalent' expression by a quite different route. It would be the solution of a different imagination to the original aesthetic problem. Insofar as we *depended* on a system of grid-reference for our apprehension of the picture, then the picture itself could tell us nothing in expressive terms. The forger needs to be a meticulous craftsman, but it is doubtful whether he can afford to be an artist as well. Here his art would only get in the way of his craft.

Wittgenstein binds this example into a wider discussion of the criteria for replication, and the meaning of 'equivalence' in expression, in which at this point – that is, the *Lecture on Descriptions* – the most pervasive model he uses is that of gesture:

> Suppose I make a gesture and I think the gesture characteristic for the impression I get ... [Mr Lewy] might have to make an analogous gesture. His muscles, hands, etc. are differently shaped. So in one sense he can't copy, and in another sense he can. What are we to regard as the copy? ... If I make a gesture and you are good imitators, these gestures will have to be similar, but different; the shape of the fingers, etc., is different. The criterion of its being this gesture will be the clicking of it in you. You say: 'Not this'. To say what's similar is impossible ... each one makes a gesture immediately and says: 'That's the one'.[34]

From his previous discussion of the 'clicking' it seems that Wittgenstein's reference to it here simply underlines the point that there just is no genuine criterion for the 'same' gesture other than that we apprehend its expressive power as the same. There are no criteria for replication, and physical systems of measurement would simply make nonsense of the claim that any two gestures were, in fact, the same. As we have seen, Wittgenstein is more interested in what 'copy', 'the same', *mean* here. In the fourth *Lecture on Aesthetics* he makes it clear, through a discussion of descriptions of gestures, that description and explanation can function very differently in certain contexts from the way they function in ordinary empirical truth-grounded contexts. When he says: 'An attitude is pretty well described by the position of the body. This is a good description. But accurate? In a way it is inaccurate'[35] he is raising questions about the meaning of description. A shrug of the shoulder is not simply more concise than an account of helplessness, indifference or resignation: it is more highly differentiated, but also it is expressive where the account or description is not. The metaphor is not just more concise than the paraphrase: it is expressive in the same way that its object is expressive.

Wittgenstein also makes use of gestures as actual explanations of particular aesthetic objects or events: 'Understanding or explaining a musical phrase – sometimes the simplest explanation is a gesture'[36] and 'If a theme, a phrase, suddenly means something to you, you don't have to be able to explain it. Just *this* gesture has been made accessible to you.'[37] But here it is clear that the term 'gesture' is being used intransitively, so that questions like 'Which particular gesture exactly?' do not have prosaic or mechanical answers; we may in response wish to say no more than 'Just *this* one'. It is less clear how helpful this is, unless we secure the answer in a context where the speaker is, on other occasions, able and willing to say a good deal more. We allow intransitive answers like these only as a peculiar sort of reply from within a vocabulary that is ordinarily more forthcoming. And then they seem to be reserved for unusually intractable responses. Our experience of a theme may after all be constituted by nothing more, nothing less, than a physical gesture on our own part. But this has sense and value only as a part of a wider vocabulary of response. Here the gesture is the mode of our response. It is not an adjunct to the response any more than is a metaphor.

> The mistake seems to me in the idea of description. I said before, with some people, me especially, the expression of an emotion in music, say, is a certain gesture. If I make a certain gesture . . . 'It is quite obvious that you have certain kinesthetic feelings. It means to you certain kinesthetic feelings.' Which ones? How can you describe them? Except, perhaps, just by the gesture.[38]

Here the response is characterised as a gesture – may really *be* a gesture – in the same sense as the music. It is an articulation, but not a verbal one, and a paraphrase won't do at all. But this sort of articulation has meaning only by being supported by a vocabulary of judgements and articulations which, being verbal, can be acknowledged and shared by others. Perhaps the centrality of a certain class of present tense singular declarative sentences is indeed the centrality of a certain mode of experience. But other modes too are in business and have importance. Perhaps aesthetic experience could not be articulated if we did not have a bedrock of criterial, truth-grounded sentences, even though aesthetic experience is not articulated in terms of those sentences. But we do have those sentences, and we can articulate aesthetic experience, and there is no philosophical reason to tie the knot any tighter than that.

The remaining model that appears in the *Lectures* is the brief reference to the *gestalt* of the scripted line, contrasted with a meaningless squiggle[39] – a model that appears also in the *Inves-*

tigations in a related context.[40] Wittgenstein compares this 'look' to the curiously mobile familiarity of the human face, although the comparison is implied rather than stated. We could not tell the difference between two slightly different squiggly lines without recourse to measurement. Yet we could tell that one handscripted sentence was 'the same' as that sentence scripted in a totally different handwriting. There are different kinds of 'difference'. In the one, arbitrary, case, we look for different dispositions of ink on paper, and in the other, purposive, case these dispositions hardly matter at all – we are looking for meaning. In the one case we would resort to measuring techniques, and in the other we would simply read – a point made elsewhere by Simone Weil in her discussion of the telegram.[41] Once again, this is an activity rather than a technique, and one which we have learned by innumerable examples, applying ourselves, case by case, as it were fresh on each new occasion. (It is an important fact that we can read a sentence which has never been written before, let alone sentences which are new merely to our personal experience, of which we must encounter thousands each week.)

In drawing together these models, Wittgenstein has built up a picture of our understanding of the expressive. Indeed, this very drawing together itself relies on a kind of *gestalt*; and the argument in the present chapter often utilises case-by-case examination rather than criterial analysis. Void of criteria, this understanding has its own kinds of equivalence, comparisons, and explanations; these terms play different roles in connection with the expressive from their normal roles in a positivistic context. We learn to do this by experience, but not by rote. And each new case of the expressive must be apprehended anew, be it a face, a gesture, a metaphor, a melody. We refer back to our previous experience of expressive gestures, but we must adopt the new gesture as it were for the first time. As Wittgenstein says, 'What we regard as expression consists in incalculability. If I knew exactly how he would grimace, move, there would be no facial expression, no gesture.'[42]

Our ability to grasp each gesture is something that we develop. I have called it a lexicon or a vocabulary of judgement, and it is something that we share with others who play the same game. It is flexible and open ended, and it allows significant disagreement. But its member judgements have a security of meaning that rests on their fitting into the general vocabulary. Some judgements – some gestures – will be seen not to fit. They will be inappropriate.

In the absence of criteria, the motion of an arm, the irony of a smile, the collision of ideas in a metaphor express insights by their 'fit'. We accept them, if we do, because they tell on us – our understanding develops in the light of them. The criterion of their having meaning is just that by our participation in this family of judgement, we can ourselves be satisfied by them.

Notes

1. Roger Scruton, *Art and Imagination* (Methuen, 1974), pp. 58–67.
2. Ibid., p. 4.
3. Ibid., p. 5.
4. Philip Barford, 'The Piano Music – II', in Arnold and Fortune (eds), *The Beethoven Companion* (Faber & Faber, 1973), p. 191.
5. Scruton, *Art and Imagination*, p. 7.
6. Ibid., p. 61.
7. Ibid., p. 64.
8. Grice, H. P., 'Meaning', in *Philosophical Review* (1957).
9. Neville Cardus, Notes to Columbia recording of Horowitz (MQ 499, 1962), p. 11.
10. Scruton, *Art and Imagination*, p. 65.
11. Keats, 'Ode on melancholy', reproduced in Gittings, *Selected Poems and Letters of Keats* (Heinemann, 1966), pp. 129–30.
12. Scruton, *Art and Imagination*, p. 172.
13. Ludwig Wittgenstein, *Philosophical Investigations* (Basil Blackwell, 1967), p. 216.
14. E. M. Forster, *Howards End* (Edward Arnold, 1947), pp. 34–5.
15. Ludwig Wittgenstein, *Lectures and Conversations on Aesthetics, Psychology and Religious Belief* (Basil Blackwell, 1966), p. 19.
16. Ibid.
17. Ibid., p. 11.
18. Ibid., p. 5.
19. Ibid., p. 13.
20. Ibid., p. 6.
21. Ibid., p. 40.
22. Wittgenstein, *Philosophical Investigations*, p. 227e.
23. Wittgenstein, *Lectures on Aesthetics*, p. 4.
24. Ibid., p. 31.
25. Ibid., p. 39.
26. Ludwig Wittgenstein, *Culture and Value* (Basil Blackwell, 1980), p. 38e.
27. Ibid., p. 82e.
28. Harold Osborne, in *Br. J. Aesthetics*, Vol. 6, 1966, 385–90.
29. Wittgenstein, *Lectures on Aesthetics*, p. 32.
30. Renford Bambrough, 'Universals and family resemblances', in

George Pitcher (ed.) *Wittgenstein: The Philosophical Investigations* (Macmillan, 1966), pp. 186–204.
31. Wittgenstein, *Lectures on Aesthetics*, p. 29 (cf. p. 34).
32. Alleged in J. O. Urmson, 'Representation in music' in *Philosophy and the Arts* (Royal Institute of Philosophy, Macmillan, 1973).
33. Wittgenstein, *Lectures on Aesthetics*, pp. 38–9.
34. Ibid.
35. Ibid., p. 35.
36. Wittgenstein, *Culture and Value*, p. 69e.
37. Ludwig Wittgenstein, *Zettel* (Basil Blackwell, 1967), para. 158.
38. Wittgenstein, *Lectures on Aesthetics*, pp. 37–8.
39. Ibid., p. 31.
40. Wittgenstein, *Philosophical Investigations*, p. 189e.
41. I owe this example to Dr Donald Evans.
42. Wittgenstein, *Culture and Value*, p. 73e.

5
Perspective and Culture

For how can it be explained what 'expressive playing' is?
Certainly not by anything that accompanies the playing. –
What is needed for the explanation? One might say: A
culture. If someone is brought up in a particular culture –
and then reacts to music in such and such a way, you can
teach him the use of 'expressive playing'.[1]

In the last chapter I have talked about the way that someone who
responds to music does so because of his participation in a
vocabulary of judgements; a kind of family of judgement. Now we
want to know how this participation comes about. And there are
two levels of answers we could give. The one we have already
given, and discussed – namely, an answer in terms of the technical
facility of organising sound under judgement according to the
practice of a particular tradition. The other level of answer describes the tradition itself – that is, the collective practice and
perspective which sustains the framework for reading and understanding – for individual understanding *within* it.

In the discussion of emotion, we noticed how easily taken for
granted is the technical *facility* of organising sound, so that the
cognitive nature of a reading is overlooked, leaving an apparently
entirely emotional 'sympathetic' response on the part of the
listener. In the same way, the *practice* of organising what we hear is
itself easily taken for granted, overlooking the fact that this
depends on our participation in a cultural perspective – the
perspective within which music (and other special activities) have
the role that they do: that is, the role of the expressive. For no
object or event is expressive in a vacuum. The role of the expressive is furnished only amid many other kinds of activities, directed
in different ways: the practical, the moral, the spiritual, the
affective, the political and so on. If the expressive is a way of
making sense of the often unsatisfactory and untidy nature of
these other activities, as is sometimes claimed, then it performs
that role in relation to the other activities, and not in isolation from

them. Of course I am not saying that every expressive action must be sandwiched between correlative practical or spiritual activities; rather that this relation must hold good on a more general level for the expressive to have the *point* that it has.

There used to be a programme on the radio called 'The Innocent Ear', in which the listener was invited to tackle a piece of music without the benefit of verbal 'programme notes' as it were. This was supposed to be extraordinarily taxing and stimulating. However, 'tackle' in this sense merely meant to supply, as if in a game or a quiz, the sort of information (composer, historical period and so on) that one would ordinarily get from the announcer. It is instructive to see how cautious and limited this game really is. It was taken for granted, for example, that the tonal system of the music would be entirely familiar to the 'innocent' ears which were tuned in around the country. Indeed, there would be no dispute about the nature of the activity in question, no problem in recognising instrumentation or formal structure; nobody was being asked to locate the purpose of this particular assembly of musicians, nor seriously to challenge which part of the presented sound was 'expressive' (it all is – that's part of the convention). In fact, the 'innocent' ear is 'innocent', if at all, in only an extremely attenuated sense, having been nurtured long since in all the larger aspects of the nature and purpose of the presented sounds. Indeed, it is only thereby that the listener is qualified to take part in the game. A truly innocent ear could not tackle the music *as music* at all.

As Hanslick observes,

> What a Tyrolese peasant sings, though apparently uninfluenced by art-culture, is, beyond dispute, *artificial* music. The man fancies of course that he sings as Nature prompts him, but to enable Nature so to prompt him, the seed of centuries had to grow and ripen.[2]

That is a very pithy remark. Listening to music is a very specialised and highly developed form of attending to what we hear, and the Tyrolese peasant sings only to the extent that he can return what he has taken in. Musical experience is not transparent, but highly directed. And the form that this direction takes is learned as a part of the perspective of the society that we inherit. It is my present purpose to think about the implications of this. One obvious implication is that not all societies have the same perspective. Not all societies have the same concerns with wealth and production, and among those that do, some are more preoccupied with natural cycles such as the passing seasons than are others. Not all societies are technologically bedazzled. It seems natural to suppose that the different orderings of activities within these different societies will yield different kinds of expressive activity, and indeed different conceptions of 'the Expressive'. In other words, music may not only sound different in different societies; it may actually have different purposes, or play different roles.

A second implication is that our understanding of forms of music (and of other expressive activities) will be tied to the perspectives that we in fact have. So that we cannot merely wander around the globe with rings on fingers and bells on toes, having music wherever we go. In different cultural contexts our ears will be worse than innocent; for they will already be beguiled by a way of listening that is completely inappropriate and inadequate to the presented sounds within those contexts. Perhaps then it is actually necessary to become involved in the other, non-expressive activities of a society in order to see what role their expressive activities have – and this latter itself surely seems necessary to appreciate those expressive activities, music among them. For to the extent that a society's general activities underwrite the *point* of what the expressive is for them, those other activities actually secure the meaning, the intelligibility of the expressive.

In *Culture and Value* Wittgenstein concerns himself extensively with these sorts of question. He often makes an observation that gives a more general valency to earlier and more specific remarks. Part of his discussion of musical expression in *Zettel* notes that

> If I say for example: Here it's as if a conclusion were being drawn, here as if something were being confirmed, *this* is like an answer to what was said before; then my understanding presupposes a familiarity with inferences, with confirmation, with answers.[3]

And in *Culture and Value* he extends the range of this line of thought:

> Doesn't the theme point to anything beyond itself? Oh yes! But this means: the impression it makes on me is connected with

things in the environment – for example, with the existence of the German language and its intonation, but *that* means with the whole range of our language games.[4]

Again, compare this from *Zettel*:

A poet's words can pierce us. And that is of course causally connected with the use that they have in our life. And it is also connected with the way in which, conformably to this use, we let our thoughts roam up and down in the familiar surroundings of words.[5]

Whilst in this later remark, again from the posthumously published *Culture and Value*, Wittgenstein makes clear the link between context and meaning:

If you just look at a sequence of notes and changes of key all these entities seem to be on the same level. But if you look at the context in which they exist (and hence at their meaning) you will be inclined to say: In this case melody is something quite different from what it is in that one (amongst other things, here it has a different origin, and plays a different role).[6]

And this holds true both for the differences between alternative contexts within a common tradition, and for the differences between contexts across distinct cultural perspectives. The role that is played by a melody, or by any expressive event whatever, is determined by its context. But that role is itself partly determinative of the *meaning* of the melody. And to understand it we must understand the context. And that may mean understanding the whole range of activities of a particular culture within which this form of the expressive has a place. After all, it is precisely this more general understanding of our own cultural perspective, and of the activities it embraces, which underpins our grasp of what the expressive means for us. It is only thus located that the expressive has sense or direction. Wittgenstein presses home the point with an analogy:

One says: how can these gestures, this way of holding the hands, this picture, be the wish that such and such were the case? It is nothing more than a hand over the table, and there it is, alone, and without a sense. Like a single bit of scenery left from the production of a play, which has been left by itself in a room. It had life only in the play.[7]

Another implication is that the relation between the general activities of a culture, and the expressive, is important in both directions. It seems reasonable to suppose that an involvement with the expressive in a particular culture also feeds back into an involvement with the other activities. It enriches our understanding of and participation in them. That is, perhaps, part of our understanding of the function of art. In reflecting or structuring other aspects of our life – the moral, the spiritual and the practical – the expressive also changes our involvement with them. We understand our mundane activities in terms of the possibilities of expression. For instance, an imaginative person will be inclined to look for aesthetic aspects to mundane situations, in the same kind of way that he might look for the aspects of faces in the glowing coals of the fire. When we call a man a philistine, we don't just mean that he is disdainful of certain ballads, vases and sonnets. We also mean that we will tend to be sceptical about the way he applies himself to other sorts of activities. There is a dimension of him that is lacking; and this might be borne out by the way he conducts his business dealings, or maintains his house and garden, communes with his family and friends, makes moral and political choices and so on. And no doubt this influence is symmetrical: in that someone will approach the expressive activities of his society in the way that he approaches his general dealings. It is, after all, only too easy to find people who are acquisitive and cynical with regard to art, perhaps as a Dombey might be, or sterile and analytic, as a Gradgrind.

Now given these fundamental links between a society's life and its art, it is natural to wonder whether there are relations between the actual forms and techniques of the expressive, and the forms of the society's activities. I doubt whether a general answer can be given to this question. Some activities, such as dance, have clear connections with functional movements; literature may have important links with information-giving procedures. But abstract music is, superficially, less closely tied to more primary actions. The answer, for any particular activity, will be a matter for empirical anthropology. The philosophical importance lies in the *possibility* that such a link exists between any given artistic operation and the other things people in a particular society do. John Blacking's excellent little book, *How Musical is Man?*, relates his own discovery of the importance of even the possibility of such connections, in his attempts to understand African tribal dance:

> The dance movement, the kind of musical development which the response is given, and the signals for the beginning and the end of the dance movements are all generated by the expressive function of the music. What is more, I could never have discovered this if I had not attended scores of performances of the dance in different parts of Venda, recorded hundreds of the word-phrases sung by the soloist, noted the relationships among words, dance and music, and learned the esoteric symbolism of the school. I had to immerse myself in Venda culture in order to understand this product of Venda minds.[8]

Of course this was, for Blacking, a deliberate, painstaking and methodical procedure, whereas the corresponding immersion in his own culture would have been gradual, unstudied, even haphazard, though just as sure. It was the dislocation of culture which forced him to undergo the procedure. But the fact that in our native cultures the procedure is comparatively formless and unconscious obscures its importance. It is only in the unusual circumstances of this dislocation that we are forcibly reminded of the importance of our cultural perspective. (Ordinarily we would reckon without it, to the extent that an expression like 'the innocent ear' can appear to take on a meaning and a validity which it does not have.) It was not sufficient merely for Blacking to have at his disposal a list of the conventions of Venda dance. He had to watch and listen *through* them. His thinking had to be in terms of them. But that would mean that each operation and convention would itself need to be located both in the framework of the dance and in the context of Venda culture as a whole. When we understand an expressive event, we are doing something that is very acute and specialised but also something that has in the course of describing philosophical discourse extremely wide-ranging connections. William Charlton discusses the kind of attention that we need to give to an expressive event such as a painting or a poem:

> What do we mean when we say that someone thinks in words?

Consider someone who, we are inclined to say, thinks not in words but in colours, shapes and proportions, the painter. One reason why we describe his thinking in this way is that even when it is clear he may be unable to tell us what it is: he can only show us what colours, lines etc., he had in mind by painting. But another reason is that he achieves his objectives by means of lines and colours, and his thought is deliberating what colours and lines to use. It is for similar reasons that we say the poet, even when his theme is a scene that might be painted, thinks in words. If his thoughts are clear, he can tell us what he is thinking, and, more important, his objectives are achieved by using words; his thought is deliberation how to describe, deliberation not what to do, but what to say. Roughly we may say that the operations by which a person hopes to succeed are the operations in which he thinks.[9]

Now this is a very shrewd piece of reasoning, and one which illuminates the nature of our understanding of expressive activities. And the main thrust of Charlton's conscious argument is already familiar to us as the denial of translatability between different modes of expression. But there is also this: that the operations by which someone hopes to succeed are also those by which his success or failure must be judged. And that means that we, the viewer or listener must grasp, assess and judge in terms of colour, line, rhythm, metre and tone. Our understanding is described in terms of them, not as an adjunct to our perception of them. If there were merely this accidental, cumulative link between our perception and our understanding, then we might reasonably observe the expressive movements of, say, the Venda dance, and bring our sets of expectations of the expressive to bear on them. But that is not enough – it is not enough in our own cultural context and it cannot be enough when we are dislocated from that context. Our understanding of the Venda dance comes about by our thinking *in terms of* the movements, signals and word-phrases which Blacking mentions. And these have significance only within the Venda culture as a whole. Our understanding could not be merely a technical matter of discovering the details of the operations and conventions of a particular expressive activity. For to think in terms of, to think *through* these operations we would have to understand their purpose and meaning. But that means the role they have among the other activities of the culture. And that role

can be understood only when those other activities are understood. And as Blacking describes it, this means immersing oneself
in the culture as a participant. After all, this is precisely how our
understanding of the artistic conventions of our own cultural
context comes about – why should we expect any less of a culture
that is not our own?

As a general rule, then, this requirement seems sound, and
amply illustrated by Blacking's example of the Venda dance. There
is, however, a complication, in that we can suffer a contextual
dislocation in time as well as across geographical divisions. Earlier
stages of our own social and cultural perspective may be very
different from its modern forms. And earlier stages of cultures
other than our own may exhibit a compound remoteness.

For example, a certain man may be fond of ceramic art, skilled
and experienced in his responses. Among the objects that he
studies and admires we could find contemporary European work,
eighteenth-century French porcelain, and early Greek, Etruscan or
Roman vases. It would be quite difficult to describe his standards
of assessment for such a range of examples. He has the benefit of a
knowledge of modern materials and techniques, but this may
cause him further to admire the work of those potters and glazers
who had more difficult and inconsistent working conditions. On
the other hand, such patronage might be quite inappropriate; one
could as easily argue that their work should be valued according to
the social virtues of their day, which might include limitless
patience and a ruthless refusal to issue any example which bore
even the tiniest flaw. Today, with the benefit of modern materials
and electronic supervision of the temperature of a kiln, such
consistency is rightly demanded, but easier to come by in terms of
human endeavour. We simply call it 'quality control', and that's
that.

Another complication may arise from the history of the preserva-
tion of earliest examples. On the one hand the finest examples are
most likely to survive because they will be continually treasured,
thus giving a misleading picture of the general standards of work
in a given society, and cultivating in us an undue reverence. The
problem is that history, replete as it is with iconoclasts of all
persuasions and none, suggests otherwise. It is the tawdry which
is more likely to escape with its glaze unsullied. Nevertheless, for
all this, our connoisseur at least has the advantage of a confident
supposition that all the examples I have mentioned enjoy the

common status of 'art-object'. They all come from a broadly
Mediterranean and European tradition, and the differences within
that tradition over two or three thousand years are reasonably well
charted. But we can see at once that a sceptic could complain that
even this says too much. By what right do we assume that we can
describe a unity of conception about the identity and nature of the
art-object over this broad and rather arbitrary slice of humanity?
How do we know that expressive purposes in Etruria were
comparable to those of eighteenth-century France?

But it is not my purpose to try and answer such a question. This
kind of answer is not entirely a philosophical one. It is partly a
matter of determining a satisfactory range of criteria for what
constitutes a given approach to the solution of expressive problems, and of determining what kinds of evidence may reasonably
be allowed to count either way. And in making these decisions a
very great deal of historical knowledge is involved. Rather it is my
purpose to point out that the value, validity and 'polarity' of
historical knowledge in this sense are directed concepts. They are
answers to inevitably loaded questions. In order to decide which
objects the Etruscans created for expressive purposes it is necessary to decide what those purposes were. And to decide *that*, all we
have to go on are the objects they produced. The products of this
society must inevitably be selected and edited by us for our own
consumption. Their vases are part of our handle on their world,
part of our passport. They are what we have to go on. We select
them because they speak to *us*, in our own condition. That in itself
is an intrinsic value, but it is philosophically important to realise
how limited in direction that value really is, and to remember how
cautious we must be in imputing it to them. The culture of Etruria
must be in part what we say it is, and that will be a function of
what is available to us – what has survived, among other things.
And in this, sheer chance plays its part. More disturbingly still, if
the artefacts of a given society constitute our frame of assessment
of that society, it begins to look improper to assess the artefacts
themselves. Is this vase good or bad Etruscan ware? Difficult
question. The vase is itself part of our standard of determination.
(How long is the standard metre?) The vase is itself one of the
parameters of this particular grammar. Is it itself grammatical? Is it
Well-Formed, or merely well-formed?

Lastly, can we be sure that we know what expressive functions
meant for the Etruscans? For we might be unable to legislate the

uses to which expressive objects might be put. Indeed for a suitably remote society we might not even be able properly to distinguish the expressive from the iconic. Once again, it won't do simply to assume that an anthropological answer is always possible. There is a rather narrow range of questions that can be addressed to a departed culture. And it is partly a philosophical task to formulate methods of appraising the objects they have left behind in such a way as to be aware of what we can impute to them, and what we cannot; to be cautious of merely exporting our own standards and roles of the expressive; and to understand that if all we have to go on is the artefacts themselves, those objects constitute the *frame* of our picture of the culture, and cannot easily fall within it.

Clearly, the point of contrast between this sort of case and John Blacking's encounter with the Venda, is that in the contemporary case we have the rest of the Venda culture to appeal to, in order to settle questions about the identity and nature and purpose and role of the expressive; but we cannot do this for Etruria. And the nature of the 'appeal' is precisely what Blacking has demonstrated it to be: it was 'to immerse myself in Venda culture and society in order to understand this product of Venda minds'. To the Western ear, the wailing of the *muezzin* from the roof of the mosque, or the insistent quarter tone of the sitar and the bewildering vocal portamento of the *raga* seem entirely dislocated from ordinary musical vocabulary. A European may make nothing of the calling of the faithful to prayer simply because he is not equipped to distinguish the direction and structure of the sound he hears. If there are notes, he is not alerted to them because they do not fall into regular divisions of the sort he has learned to handle. He is so unfamiliar with this way of organising sound that it does not, perhaps, occur to him that the sound is being organised at all. Not only does he not speak the language, but he does not speak any kind of language that uses inflection or intonation in this way. These are not gestures that mean anything to him. As Blacking notes: 'because sensory discrimination is developed in culture, people may fail to express any distinction between musical intervals which they can hear, but which have no significance in their musical system'.[10] So the Western listener may hear the intervals in the call to prayer, but fail to mark them, to make anything of them. They are as inaccessible as Arabic script – perhaps more so, because we can at least *infer* – modest achievement though that be

– that the unintelligible marks have glyphic value; they look like something that could be script. But Islamic melody – if melody it be – does not display to the European ear sufficient of the hallmarks of what we understand melody to be. (It would be interesting to contrast this case with some of the excesses of the avant-garde edge of European music, where the typical European ear might suffer a similar failure to hear music. In this instance the failure could still be an indictment – but this time, of the music, rather than of the listener.)

Perhaps slightly more accessible than the call of the *muezzin* is the Indian *raga*. Imagine a chamber music devotee listening to a *raga*, authentically performed. The *raga* has certain reassuring characteristics. To begin with, the instrumental ensemble have a clear role as a counter-melodic accompaniment. Some instruments are obviously concerned with pitch systems rather than with rhythm. And there is a meticulous organisation of the whole. But the pitch system does not seem like a coherent and reliable ordering of tones. Indeed, 'tones' already says too much, with inflected or accented quarter tones more in evidence than the semitones from which the very description of tonal music is derived. Perhaps the cyclic nature of the ululations of voices and strings suggests a melodic sequence, but no more than suggests, for that tonal organisation which supplies the European ear with a reliable set of landmarks on which to hang the idea of 'melody' is lacking. The listener might spend so much time trying to figure out the pitch system that he could never be quite sure whether he is hearing discrete parts of a single chain, so the cumulative effect of a repeated cycle is lost on him. And even if he can manage to identify the cycle, what does he make of it? What does he know of the purposes, the cumulative psychological power of the cycle unless he participates in the other, non-expressive activities of the Indian life within which this system of pitch organisation, and this adherence to a cycle have an expressive power and purpose? Nevertheless, it remains open to him, if he has the time and opportunity, to make this transition. The grammar of the Indian 'expressive' is available in the Indian life. If we participate in a sufficient range of the Indians' other activities we may build the rightly shaped place that is uniquely satisfied by the *raga*. If we do not do this then we can neither understand the music nor really *hear* the music in the *raga*, only entertain the supposition that that is what it must, presumably, be.

Now if we turn back to our own musical culture, it is perfectly possible to confront the same dislocation. In terms of harmonic vocabulary we still enjoy a virtually seamless understanding of the music of Bach's *Magnificat* all the way down to Britten's *Peter Grimes*, but this in itself does not guarantee that, for instance, we hear Baroque music with Baroque ears. I have indicated in earlier chapters the limits that I think should be placed on extra-musical association, particularly on excesses such as that offered by Deryck Cooke; namely, that there is a musical vocabulary standing in close relation to an emotional vocabulary. Nevertheless, very general connections between the form of musical expression at a given time – say, the Baroque period – and collective contemporary attitudes will be important, and relevant to our understanding of that music. It is obvious that the harmonic vocabulary of Bach is intrinsically accessible to us now (indeed, it is the basis of rock and roll) but whilst that is an important guarantor of our listening – perhaps the primary one – it does not rule out the possibility that in some relevant sense we hear differently today. Once again, our best available evidence for the nature of the expressive among Bach's generation is the works they have left us; and perhaps the wealth of music still extant (and what is more still performed) and the clear progression up to and beyond that music amply justifies our confidence that we understand it. We know what is going on in the music because we perform it, and because we perform more recent music where we discern similar, though subsequently evolved enterprises. In other words we occupy a place in a discernible tradition, and we can see with hindsight how that tradition has been extended – a vision not available to those writing and performing at the time. So this hindsight in itself constitutes an important difference between how Bach's contemporaries heard the *Magnificat*, how his champion Mendelssohn heard it, and how we hear it today. We know what it prefigured, and we cannot help hearing it in the light of the possibilities which it contained, and which we know to have been realised.

While distancing himself from Deryck Cooke's thesis of universal musical figures for specifiable emotions, John Blacking cautions against the kind of unbroken musical tradition that I have suggested. But he does so on the grounds that no universal emotional significance exists for any given musical figure:

The musical conventions of the eighteenth century stand be-

tween the Gibbons madrigal and the Tschaikovsky symphony. . . . And so I find it hard to accept that there has been a
continuous musical tradition between England in 1612 and
Russia in 1893, in which certain musical figures have had
corresponding emotional connotations. The only justification for
such an argument would be that the emotional significance of
certain intervals arises from fundamental features of human
physiology and psychology. If this is so, some relationships
between musical intervals and human feelings ought to be
universal.[11]

Blacking correctly points out that no such universal relationship
obtains and gives a counter example to prove it. But as it stands,
his argument is defective in that it is not necessary for there to be a
universal musical symbolism of emotion for such a symbolism to
be held in common across three centuries and within the confines
of the northern edge of a single continent whose cultural developments have been comparable in many other respects. The fact that
his counter example comes from a twentieth-century study of an
African tribe only highlights this *non sequitur*. Nonetheless, his
assertion that no continuous musical tradition *involving a correspondence* between musical figures and emotions has obtained
across Northern Europe could still be correct, even if it does not
follow from his premisses. I would be inclined to agree. But this
does not entail that no unbroken tradition of any kind has
obtained, merely that such a tradition does not involve the sort of
spurious emotional codification that Cooke offers. In distancing
himself from Cooke, Blacking has taken Cooke far too seriously.
The common tonality that binds Gibbons's madrigal, Bach's *Magnificat*, a Tschaikovsky symphony and a Britten opera is a more
powerful argument in favour of such a tradition than is the absence
of an assigned series of emotional connotations an argument
against it.

We have not, however, exhausted the difficulties in describing a
continuing and evolving tradition, and to these we shall return. It
is in any case apparent that Gibbons's madrigal is nearly as far back
as we can go in our own tradition before we find the harmonic
vocabulary breaking down into less readily describable features.
And indeed, we soon find that the diatonic template which is the
foundation of the harmony of Bach and of the Beach Boys is no
longer adequate to enable us to hear what is going on in the

ancient modes which were the precursors of the diatonic scale – queasily familiar yet disturbingly alien to our ears. We need only listen to Gregorian and Ambrosian chant to hear what pain attended the birth of the diatonic scale. Of course, it is perplexing to confront pre-diatonic music with expectations of the well-tempered kind. These early musicians did not have the same obsessions with dissonance and resolution that we have. They did not know, so could not be fascinated by, the full triad and its inversions, or the triadic implications for the direction of melody. The ancient modes simply do not underpin the same complexity of intervals that inform our own diatonic listening, and so could not unleash what we imagine to be the only kinds of tunes worthy of the name. So, with what understanding do we now listen to the old modes? What do we hear?

This is what Robert Simpson, writing on the slow movement of Beethoven's A minor Quartet Op. 132, says of the great diatonic champion's excursions into modality:

> The classical ear (and our own) can never be sure that it hears the old modes as their creators did – classical tonality breeds almost ineradicable habits, instincts if you prefer. Schoenberg might blot them out, but an ancient mode has too many things in common with a classical key for that. Otherwise Beethoven would not have been able to move at all from the Lydian F to the classical D major for the contrasting material; . . . and the strange convalescent lightness of the Lydian mode as Beethoven uses it is probably not a sensation that would have been felt by Palestrina – on our ears (and, I think, on Beethoven's) its effect is due to the fascinating gentle pull of the classical C major, from which we cannot and should not try to escape by a conscious effort to archaize our habits.[12]

Simpson has called on philosophical as well as musical insight here. The old modes naturally have a kinship with the diatonic scale that is not shared by Oriental pitch-inflection sets. But equally we should insist that the strange tension and unease, which arise out of expectations provoked and then merely by-passed by the modes, show that the modes and the diatonic scale are responsible for markedly different directions and potentials in our listening. Indeed perhaps there is, after all, a kind of transcontinental, and monastic, kinship between the ancient chants and the cyclical and almost arhythmic and anarchic complexity of some Eastern pitch sequences. More importantly, Simpson draws attention to what he calls our 'ineradicable habits' or 'instincts', reference points which dictate the whole structure of our listening perspective, from the effects of which 'we cannot and should not try to escape by a conscious effort to archaize our habits'. We did not drum up these habits overnight and we cannot arbitrarily exchange them for an alternative set. They dictate as well as inform how we hear. It is possible that there is some attenuated sense in which we can choose which sets of expectations to allow into the forefront of our minds, and which sets to suppress, all within some larger matrix of presuppositions. This would facilitate our listening to different schools within the diatonic tradition, or to different influences upon that tradition or upon the direction of its development, and might well resemble the kind of choices we make when we attend to this or that aspect of what we perceive. But it is clear that if we can choose at all, we can choose wrongly. And in any case this would not genuinely amount to hearing with other people's ears, if for no other reason than that deciding to bring to the foreground this or that set of expectations is a decision made within an overall perspective which is itself ineradicable. (Just as the judgement that a work is ambiguous between two alternative interpretations is itself yet a third interpretation, standing in need of justification quite as much as either of the two between which it pretends to mediate.)

We cannot get into the heads of our ancestors; consequently, we must infer rather than simply inspect what 'expressive' meant for them. And inevitably this inference proceeds out of what 'expressive' means for us. To acknowledge the perspective, and to recognise the choice between sets of expectations which is required of us, is perhaps the most we can do. Perhaps we can, in time, *adopt* the perspective of the Indian, or of the Venda, so that we really listen through it and not simply to it. But this means living their life. It is in this respect, then, with all the implications for fuller understanding which are carried, that a cultural dislocation of geography and a cultural dislocation across time are so irreducibly distinct.

Let us now look more closely at some of the ways in which this dislocation affects our understanding. Perhaps the most obvious area is that of language. One feature of the expressive is that it often involves a distillation of other areas of experience at which it is directed, or to which it refers. Not all those who use and understand language can understand sentences that are primarily metaphorical, and not all those who can use metaphors can move freely amid the poetry of the language. Not all who use a language can engage in its literature. Not all those who use bodily movements and gestures can understand dance; not all who sing for cheer and exuberance can enjoy the *lied*; not all who build can admire architectural elegance; not all who look at the countryside can read a landscape painting, and so on. As the common process of communication surrounding all of these, language is intimately tied to them all. It is for this reason, I think, that Wittgenstein uses the model of languages and of sentences within a language for so much of what he has to say about music, and, indeed, vice versa. For instance:

> Understanding a sentence is much more akin to understanding a musical theme than one might think. . . .[13]

> There is a strongly musical element in verbal language (a sigh, the intonation of the voice in a question, in an announcement, in longing; all the innumerable gestures made with the voice).[14]

Certainly it is in the expressive that language itself is at its most acute: it is partly definitive of metaphor that it is always used for expressive purposes, and is an inherently expressive device (or, as Charlton put it, used for the purpose of 'securing an aesthetic advantage'). And consequently since any perspective is dominated by its language, the fine differences between perspectives are at their most acute in the expressive uses of the languages concerned. And this is a phenomenon that can be seen across different languages themselves. Equally, what separates us from our ancestors is partly a matter of language, and the remainder – the different ideas and circumstances – are either referred to in language or (like politics and philosophy) essentially expressed through language. You could say that what is important about the differences between different generations can be found in their respective literatures. And gulfs of perspective will be at their most acute and their most poignant in the expressive.

In locating expressive judgements within the perspective of a given culture, we are saying something important about the nature of aesthetic disagreement: when two listeners arrive at contrasting readings of the same work, their disagreement is meaningful precisely because they share a common cultural perspective. If their judgements were located in different perspectives, we could not say that they conflicted because we could not say that they bore upon the same object. The entrenched Westerner who finds that an Indian *raga* lacks structure is not in *disagreement* with the native Indian who sees the structure in its transparency: they do not disagree because in an important sense they are not listening to the same thing. The Indian is listening to a form of development that is obscure to the Westerner.

By corollary, when we come to examine certain disagreements in judgement, we also illuminate the tap-root of critical judgement in a cultural perspective. Consider the case where we disagree with the views of serious and intelligent musicians writing from within our own broad cultural tradition. In this example I characterise the tradition as being that of Western classical diatonic music: a broad but widely recognised perspective, from which have sprung the musical works and critical responses that concern us in this essay.

One of my own favourite recordings is Fischer-Dieskau's 1975 account of the Eichendorff *Liederkreis* of Robert Schumann. Fischer-Dieskau himself is an *aficionado* of the regrettable view that music is the expression of emotion, and he characterises Schumann's art thus:

> The foundation on which his music rises is a purely lyrical emotion, but like the literary model this emotion in Schumann is not exhausted in aimless undulation; it is organised, rather, with an eye to concrete, clearly delineated situations, until the attainment of that distillation in form and content which Schumann always designated the 'poetic' element in music. Romanticism, as Schumann understands it, is the response to that poetic element and its need to be expressed in a music which discharges heightened artistic experience.[15]

This is bad enough already, to my mind, but these views are accorded a specific application in the notes to the recording. Writing an appreciation of Fischer-Dieskau's art, the critic Wolf-Eberhard von Lewinski considers that 'The manifold figures and scenes of the *Liederkreis*, with all their attributes, come to life with such plasticity and immediacy – with such "Romanticism" in short – that our "artistic experience" is indeed "heightened".'[16]

My own response to the songs which make up this cycle is very different; I find myself immersed in the rhythms and the continual denials and immediate reaffirmations of key centres so characteristic of Schumann. Knowing the scores reasonably well, my listening is constantly engaged in an attempt to penetrate to the centre of the sounds – the hearts of what I think of as pulsing crystals. Rather than regarding these miniatures as casement windows onto solid, animated cameos as von Lewinski commends, I am constrained to the reverse; I retreat from the world of the visual and the plastic into the cunning abstractions of Schumann's restless, shifting accompaniments, and his impulsive, often fragmentary vocal lines.

But it will be objected that my own understanding is demonstrably deficient, for I seem to ignore the relationship between music and text, surely a principal factor in approaching Schumann, who in his choice of texts was extremely fastidious. And it is true that I am bringing to bear on this music an essentially non-literary engagement; I listen essentially as a pianist, not as a singer nor yet as a dramatist. However, it seems to me that this non-literary engagement could be defended by a convincing characterisation of Schumann's *results*, as distinct from his enterprise. In drawing attention to the peculiarly pianistic articulations of the accompaniments (each in itself a pianist's joy to play) I could demonstrate the crucially melodic contributions of the piano's role, in counterpoint as well as in harmony with the voice. I could emphasise the exquisitely pointed structure of musical treatment in, for instance, 'Mondnacht' (the fifth in the cycle) where the text suggests no particular structure at all. This would encourage a specifically *tonal* approach to the work which relied not at all on literary reference.

Although I believe such a defence could be mounted convincingly, it would nonetheless be vulnerable to a serious criticism: that as I am not a native speaker of German I cannot properly weigh all the relevant ingredients in what I have called Schumann's 'results', and therefore cannot build a reading of the song cycle with any authority. I have no grasp of the pertinent literature, and thus one at least of the crucial cultural linchpins of this work is denied me.

But of course what this criticism really amounts to is this: that I have not properly characterised the relevant cultural perspective. Indeed I have appealed to a perspective which is so general (that of Western classical diatonic music) as to obscure the connections between particular music and a particular language and its literature – connections which are decisive in any understanding of the richness of Schumann's achievement.

We might think that it is only in the case of music which has an integrated verbal element (such as the *lied*) that so specific a cultural perspective is invoked. But even in instrumental music there are important connections between the rhythms of verbal language and the rhythms of melody. Wittgenstein again:

> Doesn't the theme point to anything beyond itself? Oh yes! But this means: the impression it makes on me is connected with things in the environment – for example, with the existence of the German language and its intonations, but *that* means with the whole range of our language games.[17]

... of which the obverse is that the immersion in the 'environment' – in the German language, its intonations and the language games of the culture – is distilled in the way that a German might interpret the music. Wittgenstein's concerns are typified in what seems at first to be an extravagant image: '"Fare well!" "A whole world of pain is contained in these words." How *can* it be contained in them? – It is bound up with them. The words are like an acorn from which an *oak tree* can grow.'[18]

The expectations which are incurred by saying 'Farewell!' (*Lebewohl*) and by responding to it are being compared here to the whole sum of experience and understanding which underlie the power of the phrase in any given situation. The word grows out of them, fruits on them as the physical acorn fruits on the branch. Words have their expressive power in their role among the whole set of ideas, expectations and responses: that is, among the set of our language games. It is the richness of this expressive power which makes the connections between a particular music and a particular literature interesting and important.

For instance, Beethoven wrote the first movement of his op. 81 Sonata (E flat major) around a three-note motif, mi-re-do, expressing the syllables *le-be-wohl* – farewell. Purists unanimously object to the popular rendering of the title (Beethoven's own) in the French – 'Les Adieux' – on several grounds. The French is less intimate in the personal sense than the German (surprisingly, perhaps). *Lebewohl* is, literally, fare-thee-well. Additionally, the syllables of the French do not fit the motif; *a-di-eu* is grotesque, and *les-a-dieux* meaningless in this context. The falling phrase mi-re-do is expressive only under certain conditions; i.e. when it is heard as such, as a special part of the diatonic scale, and when it is tied to what we know of the inflections and tensions in that scale. But in an important, though general, sense, this is itself tied to things in our general experience. Wittgenstein put it as: 'the existence of the German language and its intonations, but that means with the whole range of our language games'. Does this mean that the European or diatonic listener who happens not to speak German will miss the point of the sonata? Well, certainly he will have a diminished psychological response to a *part* of the point, and to the extent that this is essentially directed at the form of the motif and its subsequent development, then this is a genuinely aesthetic disadvantage.

> And yet again there *is* a paradigm apart from the theme, namely the rhythm of our language, of our thinking and feeling . . . and the theme, moreover, is a *new* part of our language, it becomes incorporated into it; we learn a new gesture.[19]

Sufficient connections simply do not obtain between mi-re-do and the inflection of *'adieu'* or the meaning of *'Les Adieux'*. The theme is not a gesture of either.

Additionally, of course, *'lebewohl'*, *'adieu'* and 'farewell' are expressions of distinct general mental sets, overlapping in many important respects and diverging in many others. That 'whole world of pain' which is bound up in the English 'farewell' is not that world which is bound up in the French or German. The difference lies not, trivially, in the immediately observable behaviour of different groups of people variously taking their leave (although clues might be found even there), but rather in the different sets of expectations that are brought to the different minds in each case. Different resonances, rhythms and alliterations: different *literatures*, embodying different sets of attitudes and ideals. It is no objection to complain that these differences are primarily important only to those who happen to be gripped by the literature and music and philosophy of a particular language and its inheritance. For these are precisely the people for whom the expressive power of the falling three-note phrase, the mi-re-do motif, will be important.

It is precisely when we *do* invoke the connections between language, sets of expectations and ideals, music and literature that expressiveness becomes important to us at all. And it is here that the fine differences between one social and cultural perspective and another are at their most acute – a point amply illustrated in this, from Philip Barford's study of the links between natural processes and the compositional process:

> German metaphysic has always seemed to be attracted towards the analysis of experience in terms of some inclusive, determinate idea. The very structure of the German language expresses this tendency. Hence German philosophy often seems to be an involved analysis of certain basic concepts intuitively arrived at in the first instance. . . .
>
> The important point is that clear logical connections can be traced between the way modern analysis approaches a musical score and the way Goethe applied himself to the study of nature. These logical connections are distinctly German. That is, they have unfolded in the German mind, and only recently spread outwards into the musical consciousness of other cultures.[20]

Whether or not Barford is correct in detail is not my concern. I am interested in the fact that he is scrutinising mental sets which he regards as distinctly German, a characteristic product of the particular perspective that is 'unfolding' in the German mind. In Wittgenstein's terminology we could say that the paradigm for these logical connections is the rhythm of the language, and of the thinking and feeling of the people who use it.

What, then, *is* the 'proper characterisation' of the relevant cultural perspective? In the above examples we seem to have conceded that a listener who shares both a language and a literature with the composer is especially well-placed to respond to a work with expressive judgements of his own. But this is, of course, an over-simplification. To return to the example of the Schumann song cycle, although I might defer to von Lewinski's reading, it equally seems to me that I might not. In conceding his distinct advantage (that he shares the German language with Schumann) I may still persist with an understanding of Schumann's achievement that emphasises the abstract rather than the concrete. This would arise from my understanding of music more generally, as an expressive but not discursive art. Von Lewinski's emphasis of the concrete, I take it, stems from a view of music as discursive. The sharing of a native language is largely irrelevant to this question, on which we have said enough in earlier chapters.

From this I nonetheless conclude that the question of language is important but not decisive. The culture that I share with von Lewinski is, after all, the rather general one of being immersed in western European diatonic music. And in considering the particular disagreement over the nature of musical enterprise, it is *this* quite general culture which is relevant. The perspective within which our judgements come into conflict is that perspective which arises out of familiarity and intimacy with a whole range of musical works from this broad diatonic European tradition, within which Schumann's vocal music has its life, meaning and gesture.

Again, if I read of Schubert's *Winterreise* being heralded as 'this greatest of all song cycles'[21] my reservations refer, not to a dispute about the adequacy of certain musical phrases to sustain certain phrase forms in the German language, but to features of the cumulative power of certain kinds of melodic and rhythmic development. I refer, not to the concrete, but to the abstract. The question is not whether, as an English-speaker I am able to discern the unique adequacy of this or that melodic fragment to this or that German expression. The question is whether, as a German-speaker I would be confined to a certain conception of music as essentially solid and discursive, rather than primarily formal and abstract. It is clear that I would not be so confined, and that the question of my language does not determine my basic conception of the nature of musical expression. Many will take issue with the view that, even here in these song cycles, musical expression is essentially an abstract matter. But their disagreement will be a function of their approach to music more generally, and not of whether they are native German speakers.

Two things emerge from this: first, the perspective which underpins a particular expressive judgement, or which could be helpful in understanding a disagreement in expressive judgement, is specified more or less precisely according to the nature of the judgement or the disagreement. A judgement that employs a certain kind of metaphor (recall Cardus's remark that Horowitz's playing 'removes the dandruff' from Liszt) is necessarily rooted precisely in an idiomatic use of a particular language, indeed in a particular development of humour. And it follows from this that the more nearly idiosyncratic a judgement becomes, the more narrowly we should have to define the perspective which underpins it. But expressive judgements may be idiosyncratic, not merely because they employ essentially personal language, but because they express a highly personal reading of a musical work. In this case the relevant perspective itself appears to become almost idiosyncratic. Here we have travelled well beyond that notion of a 'culture' with which we began. Recognising this, we must postpone a closer investigation of this more exclusive perspective until our final chapter.

The second consideration to emerge from an investigation of the role of language is this: that to ground an expressive judgement in a cultural context is to say what makes such a judgement possible, not to determine what such a judgement must be. The *cultural* perspective underlying a judgement (in contrast with an idiosyncratic perspective) gives us the necessary conditions for expressive judgements of a certain kind, but not sufficient conditions. If such a perspective were to determine the content of expressive judgements, then ultimately all disagreement in judgement would be resolvable, and the possibility of radical, persisting disagreement in judgement would disappear. But experience tells us that this is not how things are.

To be immersed in a culture is to enjoy a certain *range* of expressive possibilities, in the kinds of things we are able to say and, integrally with this, in the kinds of aspect we are able to read into music – in the kinds of listening we are able to do. The actual judgements we make are engendered and constrained by the bounds of our culture, but they are not precisely determined by them. It follows that within a given cultural perspective, radical, persisting disagreement is possible – as we know it to be.

We have settled that the perspective of a given culture is integral to the identity and the intelligibility of its music, and of the readings and the expressive judgements that are made in response to that music. Furthermore we have seen that identifying a culture is partly a matter of settling on the degree of specificity that is appropriate to the kinds of reading or expressive judgement that we are considering. Settling this is not always straightforward; indeed a disagreement in judgement (as in the case of the *Liederkreis*) may run parallel to a dispute over the appropriately specific perspective. But the identity of a cultural tradition is puzzling in another way as well: cultural traditions develop and are extended over time. Our own distance from pre-Baroque music – which we nonetheless believe we understand – shows this amply. The process of development is one in which changes and extensions are made, yet the identity of the tradition persists to the extent that we are able to say 'These are extensions and develop-ments *of this same tradition'*. Yet it is clear that developments in a tradition challenge as well as change it.

By this I mean that what comes after must supplant what went before – in a sense it must overthrow it as well as build on it. For the remainder of this chapter I propose to look at the implications of this sort of development for the identity – and, more difficult, for the self-awareness – of a given perspective. The examples I shall look at come from the developments in western European music. For example, chromatic harmony in late Romantic music is often a self-conscious challenge to the classical dominant and sub-dominant hegemony over melody; atonal music is a philosophical challenge to the diatonic; aleatory music challenges the nature of the compositional process and the status of the work itself, and so on. Each development in a tradition arises from a feeling that the existing tradition is somehow inadequate to the expression of new ideas, and that new forms or modes of expression must be developed. The interesting thing is that it is the existence of the tradition, its perspectives and its constraints which enable these challenges to take place at all. A challenge cannot occur in a vacuum, any more than can a single isolated expressive event. The flight of a bird aims to overcome gravity, for a time, but without gravity the bird's wings would not work; they would generate no lift. Indeed, 'lift' would have no meaning, because it is partly defined in terms of the downward tug of gravity. And by the same token the idea of the challenge would have no meaning apart from the constraints of the perspective within which it struggles – an analysis given by Winch[22] pointing out as he does that challenges, for example, to authority are coherent only within an authority system, so that authority is what *sustains* protest in a conceptual sense.

Once again, our discussion is best served by an example. The point of departure can be the mi-re-do motif of the *'Lebewohl'* sonata. The power of the falling phrase is a function of the intervals between the notes, rather than of the pitch of notes themselves, in which timbre and duration alone can have expressive power. And indeed this is true of all melody – it is the interval (a function of the pitch) which is important rather than the notes taken in isolation. Thus it would seem that in diatonic melody, as opposed to Eastern melody, what is crucial is an assigned, regular and recursive value to the system of intervals that make up the diatonic scale. The physical structure of a regular keyboard seems to confirm this. The value of each semitonal interval appears as though it ought to be the same, so that mi-re-do will be a constant, regardless of key or of register. In fact the measurable and mathematically describable differences between equal temperament and mean temperament show that this is not so even on the mechanical intact keyboard. With strings or voices, with reeds and with slides, intonation of any note is always at the whim of the performer. And whilst the notions of being 'out of tune', sharp or flat relative to the note seem to indicate that 'the note' has an assigned value, this is not, in fact, true. The note has an optimum value, and the permissible spread of frequency differs from point to point in the scale. Some notes are more critical than others, and at some times more than others – a point often difficult for the pianist to grasp. 'Bright' thirds and sixths are often used by the vocalist or the string player for expressive effect in certain melodic or harmonic contexts relative to a work's overall structure, and in such structures relative to the place the work holds in the developing musical tradition. Can we define from these considerations a mean value for a major sixth or a major third? In one sense yes, and the mean tempering of the keyboard depends upon it; furthermore we would also confront the question, by reference to what is this or that major third or sixth 'bright'? Yet in another sense we cannot, in that the criterion for intonation in performance is simply that the expressive value is the value which is most satisfying in an unrepeatable context. This is part of the impossibility of learning expressiveness by method or by rote.

What is more, these considerations actually affect piano performance, where it would seem that the pianist has no ability to influence the intonation of any note. The Schubert Impromptu in A flat op. 90, no. 4 is a curious and ambiguous work. And the expressive power of the central trio-like section has for long perplexed me. Why is it such a challenge to the control of the pianist? Because, in part, the nodal G sharp on which the trio is constructed (spelt A flat in the overall key signature, hence the enharmonic importance of the relation of the trio to the substantial movement) is perceived as variable. It needs to be heard as at least four distinct notes, yet the same black key must be depressed. By varying the attack and the intensity of the note, the pianist is being asked to reflect a feature of unfretted strings – variable intonation.

The tremendous power of this ambiguity is brought out first in the transitional couple of bars leading to the trio (that is, first approaching the enharmonic change): the A flat appearing as a tonic over the accompanying first inversion of the seventh chord of the tonic becomes, in the course of these two bars, almost a leading note. In the next bar (the first in the trio proper) it is the fifth of the new tonic chord (C sharp minor) and is repeated (beginning of the next bar) as the springboard of a new phrase leading to the dominant – of which it is now the ground note. Its intensity must be increased subtly each time; but the effect is not so much a dynamic one – one merely of becoming louder – as actually of altering its perceived intonation. It is a 'sharper' note altogether at its reinstatement above the new tonic in the fifth bar of the trio, and yet the same black key has been depressed.

Then, in the second stage of the trio, a sequence of three descending minims on descending octaves of G sharp return us to the 'original' note, this time appearing as the fifth of the tonic major, and the character of its appearance in the analogous phrase (leading to a passing dominant in the subsequent bar) has been totally transformed. If this were played by strings, the actual values of the successive intonations should be subtly distinct. As it is, we ourselves invest a single black key with properties which, played in isolation, it manifestly cannot have. The performance on the piano refers outwards to expressive powers which we hear and import from a wider context, that is, our immersion in a range of tonal events, of which only some can be accomplished at the keyboard. Extraordinary though this exercise may be, it could of itself occur only within the constraints of the diatonic scale as a whole. Bright thirds and sixths are still thirds and sixths; and even though intonation in performance cannot be mathematically de-scribed – certainly not prescribed – it is the existence of limits, or tolerances of intonation that give these slight but important variations their coherence and their purpose – it is the constraints of the diatonic scale which make these small protests possible. Of course, in this nineteenth-century example, the diatonic scale is not seriously threatened – it breathes out a little, and that is all. But in the twentieth century things are less certain. And the 'blue' note is a more savage protest. Once again it is particularly major thirds, sixths and sevenths which are the most yielding patients of the 'blues' treatment, again within a standard diatonic context; a fact which seems to support Constant Lambert's characteristically and omnidirectionally irreverent observation that jazz is basically the 'juicy' harmony of Victorian hymn tunes.[23] Here the blue note is the foundation of an entire musical offshoot that must be understood both on its own terms as a genre, and in terms of the diatonic tradition from which it springs. (A caveat: many hand-reared blues musicians have travelled in the opposite direction, finishing up with Haydn at the court of the Esterhazys. The trumpeter Wynton Marsalis is a good contemporary example.) So hearing the blue note as blue certainly invokes the 'straight' diatonic scale. It is only within the diatonic context that the contrast between the blue note and the regular harmony within which it writhes can occur. The essential vocabulary of blues is that of Bach; the three-chord trick is the diatonic triumvirate of tonic, dominant and subdominant, with all the wealth of developmental potential it carries (alas inadequately explored in blues and Victorian hymn tunes alike). The 'juicy' diminished, augmented and conglomerated chords of developed blues and jazz are coherent and expressive only because of their persistent reference to simpler variants of the I, IV and V chords, as anyone who hears Oscar Peterson's more self-indulgent meanderings will testify. In this context, then, the blue third, sixth or seventh has meaning only in relation to an ordinarily identifiable third, sixth or seventh. The point of the blue note is the contrast; the 'naughtiness' of being wayward.

Not *all* the notes in the scale pertinent to a given blues melody could be blue. Then we would simply have an untidy scale that was merely flat relative to the intended scale. (Just as if a company of men all step forward on the word of command to distinguish the shortest recruit; the result is that there is no shortest recruit.) The power of the blue note comes from its identity, and this is given by the 'straight' notes in the scale. When a blues singer goes too far, our orientation is sustained only by the band, whose instrumental members must exercise iron discipline in order that we not lose our tonal perspective. (Leonard Bernstein once described late Romantic chromaticism in terms of the dangers of incoherence that were latent in too wholesale an abandonment of tonal centres.) The blue note is a currency whose over-use leads to devaluation quicker than most.

What do we *make* of the blue note? Part of the answer could be that we hear the tension from the resistance to the confines of the diatonic scale, which alone supplies its coherence. To hear the blues as expressive is to be satisfied by the tension between the blue note and its original. It is more sophisticated than a simple disgruntlement with the diatonic scale. It is a good-natured side-swipe, but the blues *aficionado* is confirming his preference for the diatonic scale over pentatonic or serialist twelve-tone alternatives. What distinguishes the blues *aficionado* from the classical purist is more than a matter of technique, it is a difference in the reading of the possibilities of the scale. Additionally, perhaps, the classical purist looks for a certain harmonic order, a certain resolution and is prepared to find it at the end of a long process of key-related development. The bluesman too is concerned with order but of a different kind; he is concerned with an unattained order, yearned for more effectively through the vulgar honesty of the sensual blue moan than through the tortured chromaticism of *Tristan*. The classical purist and the blues *aficionado* take different kinds of risks in their listening. But to suggest that this can be reduced to differences of sophistication would be wrong, and insulting.

It is curious how string players and operatic singers who indulge in all kinds of intonational licence to achieve expressive effect in the performance of Ravel or Richard Strauss may still regard a blues passage as somehow beyond the pale, as anti-expressive. In both cases the challenge occurs within the authority of the diatonic. By appearing not to presuppose diatonic harmony, pentatonic or serialist twelve-tone music says nothing *about* the diatonic scale, and cannot so easily be regarded as a genuine challenge. Whereas the focus of the plaintive blue third is unmistakably the diatonic interval. Perhaps the classical purist regards the blue note as too far removed from the original to refer to it, and hence as merely a bad note, out of tune. The ambiguity is too pervasive. Hence the protest or the challenge does not register. I have already conceded that over-indulgent blue passages risk incoherence. Where we draw the line cannot be simply a matter of personal taste, for the coherence of the challenge is threatened, sooner or later. Nevertheless it must be admitted that many sophisticated musicians do not hear the blue note for what it is, and a philosophical explanation of the challenge such as I have outlined would not, I imagine, be sufficient to make them hear it.

Clearly, then, there is room for *choice*, both in our approach to listening and in our listening itself. But the kinds of choices I am describing are all of them dominated by the diatonic system itself: to protest, to challenge, or not to challenge; to abandon (as in twelve-tone serialism) or not to abandon. Protest and challenge and withdrawal, all of them, pay silent homage to a context and tradition which nurtures them all. Our technocratic society owes many debts to the Greeks, who first described the mathematical relation between a tone and its harmonies. And we place diatonic harmony alongside kinetic theory in that its constituent relations are scientific, and therefore 'real', inevitable, dependable. Whole tracts of our cultural experience are commanded by descriptions which tidy the world up in a well-ordered and properly labelled fashion. We need only imagine people who do not as a society have these obsessions to see that the inevitability of the diatonic system is a function of our perspective and culture, not of human physiology and psychology. We need only listen to Eastern music to have this 'inevitability' irrecoverably shattered.

Developments in a tradition – extensions of a tradition and of a point of view – require that the tradition be challenged, as we have said. Challenges must always be assessed against expressions that are committed to the existing context; but over-resistance to change is really no more than prejudice. The assumption that diatonic music is universally valid is a prejudice. The claim that diatonic music is uniquely adequate to western European experience is a highly committed judgement, and one which may be false, but it is different in kind from a judgement of prejudice. The problem of the extension of a tradition is that, for example, the new music needs still to be heard as music, and that seems to mean that it must hold good by many of the existing standards. Even the critic who dismissed the seventh symphony of Beethoven, at its premiere, as the work of a madman, still heard the music in it, and it is worth contrasting this case with more recent examples. It is possible to listen to some of the avant-garde excesses of the late sixties and genuinely to require the information that what one is hearing is music. And past errors can be instructive in both directions: for schoolboys do not, contrary to Schoenberg's best hopes, whistle his tunes half a century on. The question is whether the avant-garde, the forefront of a tradition, is genuinely continuous with the tradition, or simply discontinuous with it. Committed opinions – often highly committed – will incline in both directions.

Stanley Cavell brings out this dilemma in his discussion of the critical response to atonal music:

Virtually every writer I have read on the subject of non-tonal music will at some point, whether he likes it or not, compare this music explicitly with tonal music. . . . Now do I understand these comparisons if I do not share their experience of the modern? I do not mean merely that I shall not then understand what they see in traditional art. I feel I am *missing* something about art altogether, something, moreover, which an earlier critic could not give me.[24]

As a challenge to a perspective takes effect, it alters the perspective and, what is more, becomes absorbed into it. Today's ginger group is tomorrow's establishment. Consequently the committed opinion of 'earlier critics' would sound, if brought to bear on a developing situation, like prejudice. We must leave room for a tradition to expand, yet remain free to reject rogue experiments that are ultimately discontinuous with the tradition. John Wisdom tackles this problem in *Paradox and Discovery*. He tries to offer an account that would break the inflexibility of committed opinion, yet retaining its logical holdfast, so necessary to the integrity and even the identity of the perspective as it stands.

People have sometimes turned from music or painting that is new to them with the words 'It's not really music', 'It's not really art'. On such occasions they do indeed mark a difference between the new they reject and the old they accept. But at the same time it does not occur to them that the new may differ from the old not only in that it does not achieve what the old achieved but also in this, that it does not aim at just what the old attempted. They thus represent a difference as a failure. Even when this is pointed out they may still insist that this is not music or not what they call music. 'It may have certain similarities', they say 'but it's different'. And, saying this, they may deny themselves that apprehension of what they reject which they might have if they could view it not less in the light of what they accept but more freely.[25]

How we describe and how we see or hear are internally related. A change in our descriptions is a change in our vision; and a change in perspective means in a real sense a change in the nature of the observer. As Cavell shrewdly noted, in failing to share the critic's grasp of the modern he also fails to understand what the critic says of the traditional. He feels he is 'missing something about art altogether', and which could not be supplied by a critic who still operated from within the traditional perspective. A shift in perspective is pretty thorough-going:

> And a new style not merely replaces an older one, it may change the significance of any earlier style. I do not think this is merely a matter of changing taste but a matter also of changing the *look*, as it were, of past art, changing the ways it can be described, outmoding some, bringing some to new light – one may even want to say, it can change what the past *is*, however against the grain that sounds. A generation or so ago, 'Debussy' referred to music of a certain ethereal mood, satisfying a taste for refined sweetness or poignance; today it refers to solutions for avoiding tonality; I find I waver between thinking of that as a word altering its meaning and thinking of it as referring to an altered object.[26]

These are fundamental alternatives. To choose between them is to make a guess about the very nature of a shift in perspective, and about its implications. As the sonata form developed there came a point when one would have had to choose between thinking of the sonata as an 'altered object' and thinking of the word 'sonata' as having an altered and retrospective meaning, referring not to a dynamic form but to its principal ancestor. We can see the two sides of this choice in my final critical examples, the conflict between William Newman's and Charles Rosen's respective understandings of the nature of the developmental process.

Newman elaborates, in *The Sonata since Beethoven*, upon

> the dichotomy of conservative and progressive styles and forms that developed most sharply in the high-Romantic sonata between Brahms and Liszt. This dichotomy is not to be confused with the functional one between old and new, represented by the 19th century pedagogic sonatina that never left 18th century styles as against the full-scale 19th century sonata that was admired in artistic circles and played in concert halls. Only the latter is concerned in the dichotomy now in question. The actual difference ... between conservative and progressive might be elaborated as that between traditional law and order versus experimentation and fantasy. The elements and means are essentially the same but they are treated more freely and

subjectively, with a compensatory loss in dynamic tension. Thus, the melody tends to unfold continuously, in chain phrases or smaller units rather than in phrase-and-period groupings. The harmony tends toward more exploitation of third relationships, enharmony and remoter chord progressions. The passage work depends more on sequence, the ambiguity of the diminished 7th chord, and continual modulations. The tempo undergoes frequent changes, graduations and grand pauses. And because these treatments and processes operate in all sections of the sonata, not only in development sections, there is a sense of fantasy and improvisation throughout, however tight the logic behind it may be.[27]

And Newman subsequently underlines specific processes at work in the shifting of attention away from the tonal landmarks of the sonata principle:

In the Romantic 'sonata form' the tonal plan continued to function as a main means of both cohesion and tension. However . . . as the harmonic progressions and passing modulations grew more colourful and remote, especially near the era's end, the broader shifts in the tonality became increasingly dim and ineffectual as structural landmarks. In other words, the tonal plan retained its structural force most clearly on the conservative side of the dichotomy in style and form.[28]

An altered object, then, for Newman; indeed a progressively altering form. Clear tonal centres act as foci on which a structure may be hung, and consequently too subtle and intricate a tonal plan will risk obliterating the listener's sense of overall key-structure. Tonal centres may become too transitory and weak to be noticed amid the general dazzlement. In extreme cases one may be at a temporary loss to say which key-centres ought to be the nodal ones.

We can imagine an ambiguity here: a 'conservative' critic might refuse to admit the weaker tonal landmarks, and in an extreme case would conclude that the structure has been dissolved, leaving only a fantasia. A 'progressive' critic might hear in the same tonal shifts an entirely different kind of structural development based, as Newman was hinting, upon enharmonic chord relationships or verse-paragraphs of melodic fragment. The one will hear an attenuation, a dissolution, but the other an aggrandisement, of the possibilities of the sonata structure. And clearly the two will give different accounts of what the sonata form *is*. In admitting both points of view as coherent, Newman is describing a *process* at work in which 'sonata' refers to a developing, altering object. Indeed, in that he admits this process he would side with the 'progressive' critic, for he sees the development from one view to the other and consequently gives a credence to the 'progressive' which a true 'conservative' could not admit.

Contrast this with what Charles Rosen says in his book *Sonata Forms*:

> When sonata form did not yet exist, it had a history – the history of the 18th century musical style. Once it had been called into existence by early 19th century theory, history was no longer possible for it; it was defined, fixed and unalterable. Except for a few small and unimportant details, sonata form will be for all eternity what Czerny said it was.
>
> There is, of course, the history of what individual composers did with the form, but there is little continuity to that kind of history – it stops with each practitioner and starts all over again from the beginning with the next. Even its most influential exponents, like Brahms, could not change the form as Haydn or C. P. E. Bach had: after Brahms, the sonata form remained what it had been before him. There is, however, the history of its prestige.[29]

Strong stuff – but a word which alters its meaning according to the perspective of the utterer: a term of historical interest for one, a theoretical definition for another, a kind of template for Rosen himself, who nonetheless sees the word as a function of perspective.

It is difficult to see that we could defer to either Newman or Rosen solely on the basis of what we found in the relevant musical scores; indeed, it is doubtful whether they would agree to a common and sufficient set of 'relevant' scores. Theirs is a disagreement over what 'process' *means*. They are agreed on the importance of Brahms, for instance, and on the magnitude of his legacy, but not on the identity of the real inheritors of that legacy. Newman sees Brahms as part of a development that climaxes with

Liszt, a developing process within sonata form. Rosen simply does not admit such a process.

For Rosen, what permits us to talk about the 'history' of sonata form at all is just that overview which none of the Romantic masters could have had. We can see just how cellular (or otherwise, if we happen to disagree) was each exponent's manipulation of the sonata principle. For Rosen, the sonata simply could not yield to all of the various extensions and oppositions to which they variously submitted it; thus none bequeathed any change that could itself be submitted to further extensions and oppositions. And so, for Rosen the chapters of all these exponents do not make up a single story. 'The history is irremediably discontinuous because sonata form is largely irrelevant to the history of 19th and 20th century styles: it does not generate these styles, and is not altered by them.'[30]

In the afterglow of performances of the Liszt B minor Sonata by Cecille Ousset and Lazar Berman, attempts to link together these cellular fragments seem futile. But whether we choose Newman's account or Rosen's is not the point at issue. What seems to me to emerge from all this is that our view of the events in our own cultural tradition is a continually unfolding one, and each new development alters the potential and in a sense the nature of what has gone before, in that our ears are now different. We read differently from the way we read before. And this is true, it seems to me, of our extension of perspective into the art – and the life – of other cultures contemporaneous with our own. To get to grips with the *raga* we extend our perspective into the Indian's; and that has implications for how we now read our original culture and its products. Comparisons and contrasts are now available to us; not just available, but important to us as well. In discussing the Venda culture Blacking makes continual back references to products of western European music, for instance Britten's *War Requiem*. His reading of the *Requiem* is now informed by contrasts that have become important to him. His point of view, in extension, has altered. In a sense, both the alternatives between which Cavell wavers are true. The words refer to an altered object, and their meaning alters in the process.

It will be felt that this is a tautology, and so it is. The question is whether we learn anything from it. I believe we do. I believe we learn something about our responsibilities as listeners. It is part of our responsibility both to acknowledge our listening perspective and yet to *use* it honestly. The ability to take our perspective into account is bound to distance us from it to an extent, and to distance us from the expressive events that we read. So it is also part of our responsibility not to allow this to interfere with our commitment; not to become cynical. John Wisdom gives an anecdote in his discussion of our response to new and intrusive events in our musical tradition. He tells how Mr Flood, lionkeeper at the Dublin zoo, achieved extraordinary success in breeding lions through his understanding that each lion was different. 'It is not to be thought that Mr Flood, in seeking to understand an individual lion, did not bring to bear his great experience with other lions. Only he remained free to see each lion for itself.'[31] Mr Flood's continually unfolding perspective informed what he saw, but did not bind him. Wisdom applies this to us in the stricture that 'We need to be at once like someone who has seen much and forgotten nothing, and also like someone who is seeing everything for the first time'. It seems to be asking rather a lot, but perhaps the price, in terms of commitment and responsibility, attached to our understanding of the expressive is after all a high one.

Notes

1. Ludwig Wittgenstein, *Zettel* (Basil Blackwell, 1967), para. 164.
2. Eduard Hanslick, *The Beautiful in Music* (Novello, reprint of 1891 translation), p. 146.
3. Wittgenstein, *Zettel*, para. 175.
4. Ludwig Wittgenstein, *Culture and Value* (Basil Blackwell, 1980), p. 51e.
5. Wittgenstein, *Zettel*, para. 155.
6. Wittgenstein, *Culture and Value*, p. 47e.
7. Wittgenstein, *Zettel*, para. 238.
8. John Blacking, *How Musical is Man?* (Faber & Faber, 1976), p. 79.
9. William Charlton, 'Is philosophy a form of literature?' *Br. J. Aesthetics*, Vol. 14, 1974, 13.
10. Blacking, *How Musical is Man?*, p. 6.
11. Ibid., pp. 68–9.
12. Robert Simpson, 'The chamber music for strings', in *The Beethoven Companion* (Faber & Faber, 1973), p. 269.
13. Ludwig Wittgenstein, *Philosophical Investigations* (Basil Blackwell, 1967), para. 527.
14. Wittgenstein, *Zettel*, para. 161.
15. Dietrich Fischer-Dieskau, quoted in translation by Wolf-Eberhard

von Lewinski in notes accompanying *Deutsche Grammophon* compact disc number 415 190–2; Hamburg, 1985, p. 10.

16. Ibid., p. 16.
17. Wittgenstein, *Culture and Value*, p. 51e.
18. Ibid., p. 52e.
19. Ibid.
20. Philip Barford, '*Urphänomen, Ursatz* and *Grundgestalt*', *Music Review*, 1967, 218–20.
21. Edward Greenfield, Robert Layton and Ivan March (eds) *The Penguin Guide to Compact Discs, Cassettes and LPs* (Penguin, 1986), p. 804.
22. Peter Winch, 'Authority', *Supplementary Proceedings of Aristotelian Society*, 1958, 225–40.
23. Constant Lambert, *Music Ho!* (Penguin, 1948), p. 148.
24. Stanley Cavell, 'Music discomposed', in *Must We Mean What We say?* (Cambridge University Press, 1976), p. 184.
25. John Wisdom, 'Paradox and discovery', in *Paradox and Discovery* (Basil Blackwell, 1965), pp. 135–6.
26. Cavell, 'Music Discomposed', p. 184.
27. William Newman, *The Sonata since Beethoven* (University of North Carolina Press, 1969), pp. 129–31.
28. Ibid., p. 151.
29. Charles Rosen, *Sonata Forms* (W. W. Norton, 1980), p. 292.
30. Ibid.
31. Wisdom, 'Paradox and Discovery', p. 138.

6

Coda

The raw material for this enquiry was the expressive judgements made by those who listen to music. The result of the enquiry is the establishment of the *participant* listener as the fuller and more helpful picture of the business of listening to music. I think it would be right to say something about the modesty of my enterprise and of my method, in that the philosophical account of expressive judgements seems on the surface to be attractively ambitious and far-reaching.

We have seen that the interesting feature about the judgements we have distinguished as 'expressive' rather than 'descriptive' is that they do not depend for their meaning on the conditions for their truth. Indeed, they are not true or false at all as we would ordinarily understand those terms. To the extent that they are informative, their meaning has to do with differentiations that cannot be described, but only expressed: differentiations that cannot be articulated discursively but which are given by a kind of *gestalt*. And our account of the understanding of such judgements has grounded their meaning in persuasion, rather than information.

First, modesty in purpose. Tempting though it is to expand this account to cover our understanding of art-objects themselves, it has not been my business to attempt such an expansion, although I have insisted that there are important ways in which our understanding of expressive judgements is like our understanding of expressive objects and events in art. Rather what I have done is merely to look at a particularly intriguing kind of critical judgement which, employing as it does metaphor and image, celebrates and perhaps in a small way emulates the expressive activity of the artist himself. And from this I have asked what we can say about the listener. Now while this sort of judgement is an important sort, it is not the only sort, nor perhaps the dominant. Among the other sorts we should find many which stand in no need of the account of non-criterial understanding which stands at the heart of this essay. To these other, perhaps literal or technical judgements, my argument is peripheral. For instance, many judgements concerning obviously literal aspects, programmatic elements, technical structures, symbolism and representation in opera and *lieder*, associations in sacred music and so on can have straightforward conditions for their truth. It is for this reason precisely that I have not dealt with them, and not because they are in any sense unimportant to the critic's enterprise. I have looked at some of the tools in the critic's toolkit, but at by no means all. I think that the judgements we have looked at have the more philosophical interest, in not being assimilable to straightforward truth-grounded accounts of their meaning; but also more aesthetic interest, in that involving as they do metaphor and image, they have an expressive function themselves. In using them the critic is aiming at securing an expressive effect. He is participating in a similar activity to those of the artist or performer.

Second, modesty in method. For in distinguishing these judgements I have often simply noted down different aspects of their perplexity and treated them individually. I have adopted a piecemeal approach, and sometimes this has necessitated a piecemeal argument. This will have been most apparent in the crucial chapter dealing with the models for non-criterial understanding. I hope that the progression in my argument will be clear, but the approach has necessarily been discursive. I have looked at certain judgements, and at certain of their implications, located them in the perspectives which sustain them, and drawn out features of the way we understand them. I have, then, described cases but not a catalogue, and the cases that I have described do not 'form a system'. And from all of this the authority of the syllogism has remained leashed, the smack of firm generality withheld. Part of what I have tried to do is to show how a case-by-case examination of judgements can be valuable, and to secure the concept of a continuing, developing and expanding perspective without rooting it in any kind of system. I have tried to resist that 'craving for generality' against which Wittgenstein cautioned and this is inevitably as much in evidence in my method as it is in my agenda. I have made no apology for having taken my cue from Wittgenstein for much of my argument, and it seems natural, therefore, to heed his warning.

Part of the problem of generality is the temptation to lump things together under classes. Scruton, for instance, insisted on the primacy of a central class of present-tense singular declarative sentences, whose own truth-grounded meaning was supposed elliptically to account for the meaning of all other 'classes' of sentence. One of the reasons for my own rather piecemeal approach is that I see no such tidy demarcation. I do not think that all descriptions can corporately be identified as distinct from (and by implication underlying) all metaphors, only that some judgements are clearly metaphorical and that we need to look at them in order to see how it is that we understand them. And, of course, as we have seen, the minute that we *do* look we can find plenty of models for this kind of understanding. The interesting connection between metaphors and descriptions is not that one is a distinct subspecies of the other, having a specialised meaning, but rather that they both have precisely the same meaning, and that this meaning is sometimes used in connection with the conditions for the statement's truth, and sometimes not: sometimes to inform but sometimes to startle, though in either case to enlighten. It may well be true that an account of the meaning of a metaphorically used statement is epistemologically secondary to an account of the meaning of that statement used as a description, but we must resist the temptation to use this distinction as an excuse for dividing sentences up into classes, and then arranging them hierarchically. In the area of expressive activity, the expressive use of a sentence is as important as its descriptive use: indeed it becomes unclear which secures the other. There is a two-way dependence. For the purpose and the point of prosaic critical statements will often be found only by reference to poetical statements. Expressive acts and descriptive acts are both fundamental kinds of illocutionary behaviour, and it seems artificial therefore to speak of one kind as more 'primary' than the other. Better to say simply that some descriptive statements can give direction to some figurative statements, and some figurative statements can give purpose to some descriptive. In the more technocratic societies the descriptive seems to have an increasing stranglehold over the figurative; whereas allegedly 'simpler' cultures often use elliptical speech patterns in which description and imagery are intimately mingled.

It would be possible, perhaps, to see metaphor and description as co-existing in a sometimes uneasy truce; each threatens constantly to break into the other, as Gradgrind found to his cost.[1] The expressive is more than a new gloss; it is the clothes of the descriptive worn to expressive effect. But for this very reason there seems no advantage in trying dourly to separate the sentences involved into rigid classes, and certainly mistaken to distinguish descriptions as belonging to a central, primary and undubitable class of sentences, namely, those used in 'factual' statements.

In the same way, and for similar reasons, it is important not to be bamboozled into the rigid separation of fact from value. All description is tied to sets of beliefs and attitudes, because all statements proceed from some point of view or other. Descriptions are selected, arranged, sequenced and structured. There need be no self-conscious guile about this, and obviously description is not to be identified with deception. But neither need deception be absent from description, even from 'true' description and indeed a deception can easily consist solely of 'simple', 'straightforward' factual statements. It is the assumption that facts are neutral, undirected, and divorced from value which is the biggest deception of all. And the deliberate splitting off of fact from value is what constitutes the single most effective means of concealment and deception, as Joel Kovel forcefully argues in connection with the nuclear-armed state.[2] When someone says he is sticking to the facts, we may well feel that this is precisely the way he is trying to gain an unwarranted additional plausibility for that selection of facts which he is offering us, rather as the time-honoured 'unaccustomed as I am to public speaking' has grown to be an amusing badge of disingenuousness. Both the selection of facts, and the descriptions they employ, are tied to values; and by attempting otherwise, by attempting to divorce the two, we begin the deception.

It is often claimed that the camera never lies, and that what the finished print shows must be 'real' or 'true'. The problem is in determining the scope of 'true'.[3] The events that fall outside the field of view may be relevant to those within it, and the framing of that field of view is a choice which has been made by the photographer. In the same way, individual descriptions are context-related, dominated by perspectives just as are figurative judgements. How we describe depends on our beliefs, circumstances and experiences just as much as does how we evaluate or how we express figuratively. Indeed, the way we evaluate often just is the way that we describe, as when we call one building a house, and another a home. The way that we identify things in the world is often aimed not simply at securing recognition, but also at securing an assessment; it gives not just a belief, but also an attitude.

We could illustrate this by an example from discourse where objectivity is supposed to be a benchmark – namely, the defence of one scientific hypothesis against another. A scientific hypothesis will typically be produced over a period of research into a problem in which the investigator is interested. But because scientific enquiry is cumulative, and because the funding for continued experimentation may well depend on the projected outcome of the research, interest in the subject may well turn into an interest in the particular direction of the outcome of the enquiry. It is easy to construct experiments in order to yield particular results. And the goals of scientific hypotheses can all too readily be partly pre-determined. Now a scientific hypothesis is by definition open to falsification rather than to verification, and it invites the structuring of available data so that certain elements are brought to prominence and others set aside. It is the enquirer's job to produce a hypothesis which will stand up to hostile scrutiny, but too often this can mean a hypothesis which is proofed against counter-evidence. This means that the data to which the hypothesis will be readily subjected must be carefully chosen, and the remainder must be in some sense discredited as irrelevant, unreliable and so on. So part of the defence of a hypothesis is the limiting of its scope to data which will not falsify it. And this means that the defence of a particular hypothesis is really more a justification of the approach which underlies it. The defence must consist in making people accept the value of that approach, of those choices, of this way of proceeding, of the predisposition to look in that particular way. In effect then a dispute between two enquirers may be less a dispute over how to interpret 'the facts' than a dispute over which data should be identified and credited as 'the facts'. Thus, the nature and value of the descriptions which an investigator chooses and uses depends on the context of his approach, method and purpose – a context which he himself largely defines. He wants to secure agreement, not so much in beliefs concerning the data that there are, as in an attitude towards them – from which the descriptions involved in his hypothesis must follow.

One of the sources for the temptation to regard descriptions as 'straightforward' and value-free is the existence of some terms which seem to have the special job of calling up value assessments, calling attention to certain kinds of attitude. Leaving aside the obvious – and problematical – examples of 'good' and 'bad', there are in ethics, according to Philippa Foot, a whole family of concepts which not merely call attention to moral assessment but whose use actually constitutes it.[4] So that our understanding of the 'good' of ethics is supposed simply to be the approval pertaining specifically to things like loyalty, courage and integrity; whilst moral disapproval just is the sort of thing directed towards things like sloth, cowardice and deceit. As such, the use of these terms in descriptions would not merely identify a moral attitude but also constitute it; calling an action a 'theft' would not merely say that the action fell within the province of moral scrutiny but would also condemn that action, if Foot is right. Now it is not my purpose to discuss whether or not we can accept the account. But I do want to point out that if it is right, it merely extends the list of terms that can act in this particular way – that can act as specific identifiers of value. And the result, whether we accept a short list containing only self-evident terms of approval and disapproval, or an extended list of a family of such terms, is that we can be tempted to think that other descriptions which do not involve these identifiers are somehow morally neutral, or are otherwise value-free. In other words we can have a picture of 'straightforward' undirected descriptions at large, which are perfectly reliable and safe to use, and are pressed into the service of value-judgement only by the specific agency of professional value-identifiers, which are easy to spot and to respond to. And this picture seems to give credence to the splitting off of fact from value – the value is returned to the fact only by the use of agreed signals.

In resisting this view, in locating the value and direction of descriptions at large in the context of their use I wish to push fact and value back together. We can see why this must be done in considering whether there are any aesthetic identifiers of the sort Foot has claimed for ethics. Superficially we might suggest 'beauty', but apart from the fact that this is a rather short list, it is a truism that beauty is defined according to the practice of a given culture and a given perspective, and from this it follows that it is less useful than indications of the particular features and forms that constitute beauty on any given occasion. Indeed, 'It's beautiful' is primarily an interjection, as Wittgenstein points out, and much less a serious evaluation.[5] Now suppose we say that in a particular context 'coherence', 'integrity', 'purpose', are what invoke aesthetic approval. What we are doing is drawing attention to the function of the context in defining the value quite as much as to the features themselves. In evaluating a work, we shall point out those features which underwrite the work's value in that particular context, or for that particular perspective. And in drawing out these terms we will be paying tacit homage to a host of other judgements which form the background or the matrix within which those terms have the evaluative force that they do.

In the course of this essay I have made use of only one term as a consistent aesthetic identifier, namely 'expressive', since I have taken it that the distinctive feature of aesthetic activity is that it 'expresses' rather than describes. (Indeed I have even left it an open question as to whether 'expressive' must always invoke approval, in that it can be used intransitively or transitively, and where it is used transitively, it may be used in connection with features that work against the larger expressive purposes of the art-object as a whole: for instance a work that is expressive of chaos may simply not be helped by features which are expressive of unity, and so on.)

Although debased, the term 'beautiful' *can* have the function of an aesthetic identifier, only provided we know enough about the context of its use to take it seriously. But the point is that no more and no less is required of a whole variety of terms which, taken in isolation and unsupported might seem to have to do with attitudes of approval of some more general kind. For instance, thoroughness is generally approved. But in the right circumstances it could be a term which called our attention to a specifically aesthetic attitude towards a particular object or event – principally where mechanical or practical considerations were beside the point. To say that someone was thorough in choosing a name for a child could be to make something very like an aesthetic identification: it could call our attention to a sense of the 'fit' between, say, name and face. On the other hand, to say that someone was thorough in making his friends is to make something more like a moral identification. But it is the context which decides. And it is the context which restores value to fact.

Now here there is, I think, a direct parallel with identifying the expressive use of descriptions. It is the circumstances of the use of a description which show whether or not it is being used for expressive effect. Part of those circumstances will be the intentions of the speaker, another part the predispositions of the hearer, to characterise and to view things in particular ways – ways that we can come to appreciate, to expect, and to enjoy. It is my purpose not to deny any distinction between the figurative and the descriptive, but to contain it and to understand it for what it is. Equally I do not want to deny the distinction between fact and value, but rather to insist that it is only in the context of a sentence's use that the distinction can be understood, for it is only there that we can see what value a sentence might indeed have. I want to point up the futility of general and detached and bald oppositions. I want to illuminate the threatened obscurity of image – and to do that we must doubt the transparency of fact.

Now the way that we understand the judgements of others depends on the way that we would ourselves select and order descriptions of a particular object, just as the judgements that others make are a function of the descriptions they have in fact chosen. Clearly, then, agreement in judgement and agreement in description are intimately linked. The selection we make of descriptions is a choice that we make according to our perspective. We become both accustomed and inclined to bring a situation under a certain selection, and under certain kinds, of judgements. We can see this at work in different levels. Trivially, someone with a particular interest or hobby will tend to associate everyday events with the terminology of his hobby. Thus the football fan will often ask 'what time do we kick off?' when he is referring, perhaps, to a journey or to a wedding. On a different level the Christian will be inclined to see human behaviour in terms of sin or of sin redeemed. He is disposed to see a certain kind of malign agency or purpose behind individual carelessness or thoughtlessness, whereas a non-Christian (provided he was not instead a fatalist) might see no particular agency at all; the very description would not occur to him. He might see simply a random, haphazard interruption in an ordinarily purposive sequence of individual actions. A Marxist critic sees the rumblings of class struggle in Shakespeare's historical plays or in Dickens's novels, and finds no obstacle in the enterprise of the writers, even though they be inferred to have been quite distinct from any premature analysis in terms of class struggle. An atonalist musician sees late Romantic chromaticism as a liberation, and will generate and select his descriptions accordingly; the classical purist will see only decay, and the modern serialist will see something yet distinct. And so on.

It seems then that we make our critical choices, we select the descriptions in which our judgements will be framed, in advance of the actual events to which we apply them, rather as we make our moral choices – not in the split second during which action may be required without deliberation, but beforehand, in the general assembling of our priorities, our imperatives and our convictions. Against this it is sometimes said that when someone performs a courageous act, such as jumping into a canal to save a child, he thinks of the enormity of the risk only after the event, when he has time to reflect. Yet the decision to attempt the rescue was effectively taken before the situation ever arose, in his beliefs about the value of a child's life, and about his responsibility to others. Or perhaps it would be truer still to say that no such 'decision' was ever taken at all in the intentional sense. Certainly he did not deliberate at the time – he simply jumped, for had he paused to reflect he might have been too late. What galvanised him were his attitudes concerning the value of a human life and his responsibilities towards that life, including, if necessary, risking his own to save another. What he reflects on afterwards are 'the facts' of the case, namely the circumstances which give rise to descriptions about the extent of the risk he was taking. The order in which these came to him – responsibility first, risk second – show what sort of a person he is. He is someone who is likely to act in the way he did because that was the way he saw (and would have described) the situation. Someone who, prior to the situation, thought only of risks to himself, and only afterwards of his responsibilities to the child, would be less likely to act than to descend into remorse and self-pity. He would be a different sort of person, and we should see this not just in how he tended to act but also (and these are tied together) in how he would describe.

Now the way that we make our critical assessments – or indeed our very approaches – to a work of expressive value can be similarly understood. We will know from what someone says whether he will examine a work for its underlying structure in preference to its surface; he will be predisposed to do one or the other (or occasionally both) and this will be shown in the way he describes. He will tend to describe a work in terms of its structure; the importance for him of structure will come out in the things that he chooses to tell us about. (I eventually concluded in my own case that it was a disposition to examine surface rather than structure which explained my aversion to Brahms.)

We have already discussed in an earlier chapter how our seeing or hearing aspects is tied to our persuasions and inclinations – the way we set out to look at or listen to something. To say that not everyone sees or hears the same aspects in a work (or in any kind of situation or event for that matter) is really to say that not everyone looks for the same kinds of thing. Not everyone is predisposed to describe or to see in the same way, and this means that certain descriptions will simply not occur to some people, whereas for others those descriptions will be almost inescapable. Someone who has a sense of the expressive, or someone who has a sense of duty will bring under aesthetic or ethical judgement situations which might appear to have no such aspect to someone else. Of course, this sensibility, this predisposition is developed in the context of individual situations, that is, not conceptually divorced from them. But once the disposition is established it affects the way we see subsequent situations. It is the adoption of a certain way of describing, and it becomes constitutive of the way we see.

There is an important sense in which our predisposition to see in this or that way constitutes an intervention in the circumstances in which we find ourselves. We could compare the sense of the expressive or the sense of duty to having a sense of humour. We say that someone has a sense of humour who habitually sees the incongruous or ironic aspects of a situation as if they were the most prominent, and who habitually draws other people's attention to them. Someone with a sense of humour changes the way that *we* see a situation, he changes the relative prominence that the different aspects of a situation have for us. Now the perception of someone that a situation has an ironic or incongruous aspect is ambiguous. They speak as though they feel something to be funny, but the status of the funny thing just is that this is how it has been seen by someone, moreover by someone with a sense of humour – someone who is disposed to see things in that sort of way. Additionally of course, the whole operation of irony or of incongruity relies on the fact that the ironic situation is Janus-faced: it has a straightforward aspect which is trodden underfoot by the application or the intervention of humour. It is primarily because a situation ought not to be funny, that it can in fact be made to appear funny. Therefore the perception of the humorous aspect of a situation is not a belief, but rather an attitude. It is an intervention into a situation that is, *seen in another way*, not funny at all. In exactly the same way then the disposition to see an ethical or an aesthetic dimension to a situation is not a matter of belief but rather of an attitude. Somebody who displays an ethical or an aesthetic attitude towards a situation changes it even for those who do not of their own accord see it like that. Of course this change may make no difference to how they themselves subsequently describe or act, but there again it may very well do so. It depends on the availability of their own perspective to be influenced. In exactly this way, when someone imaginatively intervenes in a situation by redirecting our attention through the use of metaphor and image, he attempts to change it for us. He attempts, through what he says, to make us see differently.

People who tell jokes like to tell them to other people who will laugh. Humour at its best is collective, and laughing in fellowship is better than laughing alone. It is poor sport to tell jokes to people who do not see them, and only temporarily amusing to laugh at the humourless. We tell jokes not merely to entertain but to establish a particular way of seeing. We want others to see as we do, partly because we need, up to a point, to reinforce the way we view. And this is as true in aesthetics as it is in humour. While it is stimulating and often fruitful to strike our judgements against the imagination of someone who views an object or situation in a very different way, we need confidence to do this – and such confidence arises both psychologically and logically from our being made secure in our own perspective, partly through the confirmation of others who see as we do. The psychological need for reinforcing is obvious enough whilst the logical need arises from the fact that disagreement in aesthetics is meaningful.

There is in aesthetic judgements a kind of imperative. If the aesthetic attitude towards a given object or situation were merely idiosyncratic, of no more consequence than a preference for sweet foods, then aesthetic disagreement would not be significant, and could not be taken as seriously as it in fact is; and we have rehearsed the distinction between the aesthetic and the gustatory in earlier chapters. Aesthetic disputes do not collapse into differences of taste, and one can learn in a significant sense to be more acute in one's judgements – to make judgements which are more worthwhile.

This is shown in the kinds of defence we are prepared to make of our *preferences* in music. We begin our careers as listeners by exhibiting preferences that are perhaps naive; preferring the vigorous and the stirring to the contemplative and the architectural, perhaps, and then later preferring the impressive architectural structure to the cameo, and so forth. Furthermore there arises a development in the complexity, subtlety and power of the reasons we can give for our preferences. As our experience intensifies, as the range of music with which we are familiar extends, so our understanding of each musical text is broadened and deepened by its relocation in an ever-richer context. As our understanding is enriched, so too is our capacity to form (and occasionally to resist) preferences, and to defend them, increasingly in the context of an emerging conception of the nature and enterprise of music itself.

For example, my earlier defence of a 'formal' as opposed to a literary appreciation of Schumann's *Liederkreis* song cycle rested upon a certain conception of music as a formal rather than a referential art. In concentrating on the formal and the structural in music, I am drawing attention to certain features of the music, but only to certain, not to all. And this must be defended as a mode of interest in the musical work. The defence of a mode of interest is itself to an extent perplexing. My defence of the formal or abstract appreciation of *Liederkreis* concentrates on certain *kinds* of features – the formal and structural rather than the allusive, the referential, the discursive. These are the features to which I turn and return; they are the features in which I am interested, and by which I am satisfied.

In preferring this reading to a reading which stresses the programmatic, am I claiming simply that the greater, the longer lasting satisfaction is found in such features (than is to be found, say, in concentrating on the references to the concrete)? In a way I am saying this, but in a way I am saying more – that such satisfaction is the *only* kind available to me, and that the allusive or discursive or programmatic features are beside the point for me; I pass them by.

But this, too, I have learned to do: I have learned to pass certain things by, and to turn and to return to others. In a way this is a *choice*, but it is a choice of an elusive kind; it is in learning so to choose, and then crucially in constantly so choosing that my mode of interest in the work (indeed in music at all) is now identified and described. I have learned, through the examples and descriptions and instruction of others, to attend in this way rather than that. I have learned to see in a certain way (to recognise certain aspects rather than others) and I have learned *how to be satisfied*.

When certain kinds of features speak to me, they speak to me because I am, as it were, ready to be spoken to: but this readiness was itself something I had to learn. When the vocal line of 'Mondnacht' arrests me in the way that it does, when the semitonal clash between the voice's sixth syllable and the lingering bass accompaniment strikes me as rich and pregnant, rather than simply as misplaced or incompetent, this is because of the range of harmonic and melodic possibilities that I have gradually learned, to which I can refer, and to which Schumann's guile points me. Of course, this is not a process of deliberation; as we have discussed earlier, the fluency with which we have learned to read disguises the cognitive character of our listening, and this is as true in distinguishing that melody which is 'great' as it is in distinguishing melody at all.

Melody is, as we have already remarked, about the raising and confounding of expectations; but only certain surprises fall within the limits of intelligibility. Schumann's genius in the motivic phrase of 'Mondnacht' is noiselessly to brush, for a moment, against the darkened veil that divides melody from chaos: but to do so by means not exactly of the melody itself but of the fleeting gulf between melody and accompaniment. This limpid, velvet, rising phrase has within it an iron splinter whose presence is revealed only by the refractory power of the false bass. The unity of melody and accompaniment is re-affirmed when voice and bass together swing gently down the broken tonic chord to the interrupted cadence which ends each of the first four of the song's eight brief, languorous couplets.

Music refers to itself: this is the grounding and the manner of my reading as I have expressed it here; and the grounding and the manner also of this mode of interest in the musical work. 'Melodic chaos' refers beyond the established order of expectations; expectations arise from our familiarity with countless other fragments of melody, of which some may clearly be more central than others (I think of the foundational fragments of our melodic and harmonic vocabulary which are assembled in so many of the Lutheran chorale tunes). Again, the 'false bass' is distinguished from the proper, the familiar and the comfortable – notions which were given currency in the music of Bach, and which were as familiar to Schumann's ears as to our own, though overlaid by different subsequent resonances. We are gripped by this fragment of Schumann's melody because of what he has suggested to us and then declined. He has given us a melody of such a stamp as to proffer commentary on and insight into other melodies, actual, possible and – as it were – inconceivable. Thus 'Mondnacht' is, after all, discursive: it is a brief essay upon melody. Yet though this has taken some time to describe, it is effected of course in the single instant during which, on first hearing such a melody no less than on subsequent listenings, we are taken as it were by the throat, immobilised. Because we are immersed in the perspective of European diatonic melody, and because we have learned fluently to listen in a certain way, precisely *this gesture* becomes available to us with an immediacy that astonishes.

In maintaining this approach to the *Liederkreis* cycle, then, I am indeed expressing a kind of choice, a choice concerning the kinds of insights which satisfy, to which I could want to return, and which are made available precisely by this mode of interest in the musical work. (To be interested in the allusions and depictions of the plastic, the solid, is to read the sounds of Schumann's music in an essentially literary way. But I have passed by that other choice so often that now I do not seriously believe it is open to me to take it.)

Again, in preferring this melody to that melody, this structure to that, I am making an essentially formal choice: I am choosing on the basis of form. But reference is not ruled out; on the contrary reference is inevitable in our listening. The question reduces to the identity of what is referred to: the answer emerges as being the vocabulary of expressive fragments, compiled in the growing diatonic tradition and partially and gradually learned by each of us as we take our places among other listeners. This does not of course mean that there is somehow a *positivistic* answer to the question: Is this melody better than that? The answer may differ irreducibly among listeners, and reflects listeners' different individual melodic vocabularies, their larger preferences concerning form, structure, period, instrumentation and so on; as against this there is often wide agreement amongst listeners as to the identity of certain very great melodies (*Erbarme dich* from the *St Matthew Passion*, the lyrical second subject from the opening of Mozart's K488 Piano Concerto, the opening of Beethoven's 'Spring' Violin Sonata, for instance). It is not my purpose to adjudicate: the form of such preferences is what concerns me.

Great melody is distinguished from the mediocre by its ability to arrest and to satisfy us again and again. But this arrest, this satisfaction arises from our vocabulary of musical experience, learned as we gradually become listeners, and grounded in a core of seminal melodic fragments which have furnished the diatonic tradition. To prefer this tune to that, is to bring to bear one's individual, cumulative listening experience upon the sounds presented to us. It is to read; to read in the fluency of immersion in a given tradition, whose limits determine alike the possibilities of melody, and the range of preferences that are open to us. Only within that range do our individual careers as listeners determine the precise readings and preferences that we make.

By corollary, the preferences and readings that we make will in turn exhibit our careers as listeners. To defend a given reading of a work is in a sense to defend what we are as listeners; if we obtain others' agreement in our judgements, we obtain their affirmation of us as co-listeners within the perspective of our tradition.

So the agreement of other people to the way we see and describe is a matter of importance to us both logically and psychologically, and we deploy our judgements to that end. Conversely we *learn* our judgements with that end at least covertly in mind – we learn to be able to judge in a way in which we see others judging. In general terms (notwithstanding the Herculean determination of some brave soul to maintain an idiosyncratic isolation) there is a certain conformism about the way we adopt and adapt particular selections from what I have called the vocabulary of judgement pertaining to our society. We build up our portion of that vocabulary in conformity with an aesthetic attitude that is in part taught us and made available by example. Of course, it is precisely in the security of such a context that we are able to feel any urgency about fresh insights that we may encounter or develop for ourselves – their freshness and consequent urgency is identified by the way they stand to the broad assembly of judgements we have accumulated.

The challenge of a new way of hearing a work is underwritten by the reliability and coherence of the approach to listening which we share with our fellows. And as we saw in the last chapter, for any given context the nature of that shared approach is a function of a more general community and its other activities.

The point of the punchline of a joke is that it jolts those who can already see the relevant situation under a more prosaic set of descriptions. That is how the incongruity works. But of course the audience must also be able to see it in the new way that the joke provides, and they must learn to do this by example – though, clearly, not by explanation, for explanations always kill a joke stone dead. This, too, is a part of the general activities of a given society. Now the point of a new image is that it jolts those who can already view an expressive object or event under familiar and well-formed judgements. But of course they must also be able to see in the new way that the image provides, and they will have learned to do this through many examples, though not explanations, as a part of the acquiring of that experience-in-judgement which is the womb of insight.

There are also risks. Professional critics seem often to talk merely to one another, and this condition is aggravated when the topic of discussion is modernist theories of composition, as Cavell wryly points out.[6] Reinforcement has its perils, and the problem with humour is that the humorist too often knows exactly what he is looking for in a situation; after a while, pointing out the incongruous is not enlightening, but just narcissistic. Indeed this hazard presents itself to the philosopher as well, as one or two remarks in *Culture and Value* suggest:

> If I say that my book is meant for only a small circle of people (if it can be called a circle) I do not mean that I believe this circle to be the elite of mankind; but it does comprise those to whom I turn (not because they are better or worse than others but) because they form my cultural milieu, my fellow citizens as it were, in contrast to the rest who are *foreign* to me.[7]

Finally, we return to that perplexing implication which we have shied away from on more than one occasion during this essay. Perhaps now is the time to face it. For when an expression is sufficiently tied to the perspective and circumstances of its utterance – and when its meaning is dependent on its persuasive force – then to see the point of what someone is saying is to accept it: the gap between understanding and assent, ordinarily necessary to make room for significant denial (and hence, ordinarily, for meaning at all) is closed. When we discussed the 'dawning' of an aspect we flirted with such an account. We did so again in the discussion of the fruitful collision of ideas in metaphor. And the operation of the models of non-criterial understanding – in particular the models of facial expression and of gesture – tied recognition and interpretation together intimately, so intimately that understanding and assenting to the particular interpretation seemed to coincide. To 'see' at all in these cases is to accept the image, the face, the expression as real. The author of the image and the recipient are united, briefly, in their imagination. Their perspectives exactly coincide, and it is this coincidence that, as it were, constrains us to understand, compels us. It is the importance of sharing an insight that is newly available to us which redeems the event from the triviality into which it might otherwise fall. Peter Winch has put it like this:

> There are ... cases where we feel that a certain kind of response is, as it were, necessarily required of a certain kind of object, so that anyone who understands the nature of that object would *have* to respond in that way ... the corresponding idea in aesthetics with which I am concerned, would be that a certain picture, poem, novel, play etc., of its nature *compels* a certain response from anyone who properly understands its nature. And this is not intended as a psychological generalisation so much as a metaphysical truth. ... But there are cases where one wants to say something different, namely, that two people who respond quite differently to a work of art do *not* understand it in the same way. It's important to see that there is a certain indeterminacy about the distinction between a case describable like that, and one describable as that of two people who understand the work in the same way but respond to it differently.[8]

But the distinction need not be indeterminate, and Donald Evans's discussion of meaning and understanding shows us why.[9] It is not that the picture, poem or what have you 'of its nature' compels a certain response, it is rather that the 'nature' of the expressive object is not given once-for-all but is a function of how it is seen and understood. It is that in responding differently, two people are liable to show from their descriptions that they are not confronting precisely the same 'nature'. What they allow as the essence or nature of the work will be shown in how they describe, and they are describing differently. If we reinterpret Winch in the light of this, we can see the full depth of his insight. Anyone who understands the 'nature' of the object is *already* committed to an interpretation. Winch projects this analysis into the area of actions:

> When I'm horrified at the way someone is behaving ... I may sometimes say to him 'You can't behave like that' (which seems to assume that he doesn't understand what he is doing). But in some cases I may address him differently and ask 'Don't you

understand what you're doing?' That is, I may take his indifference to what he is doing as itself a criterion for his not understanding the nature of *what* he is doing.[10]

By corollary, anyone who does understand the 'nature' of the action is already committed to an interpretation, and through this to a certain response: for this is part of what understanding *means* here – how a person responds is part of the way we *identify* how he has understood the action.

What I wish to argue is that, though superficially circular, this conclusion is nevertheless important. By fusing recognition, understanding and assent in this way, and in this sort of context, we locate the real source of many critical disputes (such as that between Newman and Rosen). More importantly we restore the validity of an objectively supported view of a work to the intimacy and personal significance of the individual perspective. This is why we value expressive insight – for in sharing an image we share a perspective; and this means sharing 'experience' in its fullest sense, freed from the trappings of sensation. And lastly this conclusion properly frames our picture of the participant listener; for it is by *engaging* in the art-object and by committing ourselves to it and by participating in it with our imagination that we see it most clearly – and when we share our judgements with others we are also sharing that seeing and that participation.

Perhaps this is one of the fuller aspects of 'community' – to share the engagement of another mind and another imagination with the expressive object. Perhaps one of the most valuable things about the expressive is that it provides the medium and the circumstances for us to do this – to engage with one another on the level of the imagination, and overcome part of that isolation for which, as Dylan Thomas put it,

> . . . the moon rages
> And the lovers lie abed
> With all their griefs in their arms.[11]

And perhaps this is how we learn one facet of what Wittgenstein calls, in that seminal paragraph from the *Investigations*[12] 'better knowledge of mankind'. This is, after all, part of our purpose in the expressive. In describing the extension of perspectives, the participation in what we see and hear, and the fusion of recognition, understanding and interpretation, I hope to have described part of our method.

Notes

1.   Charles Dickens, *Hard Times* (J. M. Dent, 1931), especially pp. 262–3 where Gradgrind is forcibly reminded by Mr Sleary that facts and calculations are not enough.
2.   Joel Kovel, *Against the State of Nuclear Terror* (Pan, 1983).
3.   I owe this example to Dr Donald Evans.
4.   Philippa Foot, 'When is a Principle a Moral Principle?', *Proceedings of Aristotelian Society Supplement*, Vol. XXVIII, 1954, especially p. 108.
5.   Ludwig Wittgenstein, *Lectures and Conversations on Aesthetics, Psychology and Religious Belief* (Basil Blackwell, 1966), p. 2.
6.   Stanley Cavell, 'Music discomposed', in *Must We Mean What We Say?* (Cambridge University Press, 1976), pp. 185–9.
7.   Ludwig Wittgenstein, *Culture and Value* (Basil Blackwell, 1980), p. 10e.
8.   Peter Winch, 'Text and context', *Philosophical Investigations*, Vol. 5 (1982), 55.
9.   Donald Evans, *Values, Actions and the Language of Vision* (University College, Cardiff, 1980).
10.   Winch, 'Text and context', p. 55.
11.   Dylan Thomas, *In my Craft or Sullen Art*, reproduced in Christopher Copeman (ed.), *Living and Writing: Dylan Thomas* (J. M. Dent, 1972), p. 1.
12.   Ludwig Wittgenstein, *Philosophical Investigations* (Basil Blackwell, 1967), p. 227e.

Bibliography

Abrahams, Gerald, *Chopin's Musical Style* (Oxford University Press, 1939).

Bambrough, Renford, 'Universals and family resemblances', in George Pitcher (ed.), *Wittgenstein: The Philosophical Investigations* (Macmillan, 1966).

Barford, Philip, 'The piano music – II' in Arnold and Fortune (eds), *The Beethoven Companion* (Faber & Faber, 1973).

Barford, Philip, 'Urphänomen, Ursatz and Grundgestalt', *Music Review* (1967).

Black, Max, 'Metaphor', *Proceedings of the Aristotelian Society* (1954/5).

Blacking, John, *How Musical is Man?* (Faber & Faber, 1976).

Bujic, Bojan, 'Aesthetics of music', *Br. J. Aesthetics*, Vol. 15, 1975.

Busoni, Ferruccio, *A New Esthetic of Music* (in Three Classics in the Aesthetics of Music, Dover Publications, 1962).

Cavell, Stanley, *Must We Mean What We Say?* (Cambridge University Press, 1976).

Charlton, William, 'Is philosophy of form of literature?', *Br. J. Aesthetics*, Vol. 14, 1974.

Charlton, William, 'Living and dead metaphors', *Br. J. Aesthetics*, Vol. 15, 1975.

Collingwood, R. G., *The Principles of Art* (Oxford University Press, 1938).

Cooke, Deryck, *The Language of Music* (Oxford University Press, 1953).

Davidson, Donald, 'What metaphors mean', *Critical Enquiry*, Autumn (1978).

Doernberg, Erwin, *The Life and Symphonies of Anton Bruckner* (Barrie & Rockliffe, 1960).

Evans, Donald, *Values, Actions and the Language of Vision* (University College, Cardiff, 1980).

Foot, Philippa, 'When is a principle a moral principle?', *Proceedings of Aristotelian Society, Supplement*, Vol. XXVIII, 1954.

Forster, E. M., *Howard's End* (Edward Arnold, 1947).

Foulds, John, *Music Today* (Ivor Nicholson & Watson, 1934).

Fry, Roger, *Vision and Design* (Chatto & Windus, 1925).

Hanslick, Edouard, *The Beautiful in Music* (Novello, reprint of 1891 translation).

Hedley, Arthur, *Chopin* (J. M. Dent, 1947).

Hepburn, Ronald, 'Emotions and emotional qualities: some attempts at analysis', *Br. J. Aesthetics*, Vol. 1, 1961.

Hindemith, Paul, *The Craft of Musical Composition* (Associated Music Publishers, 1937).

Hopkins, Antony, *Talking about Sonatas* (Heinemann, 1971).

Howes, Frank, *Music and its Meanings* (University of London, 1958).

Lambert, Constant, *Music Ho!* (Penguin, 1948).

Langer, Susanne, *Philosophy in a New Key* (Havard, 1951).

Langer, Susanne, *Feeling and Form* (Routledge & Kegan Paul, 1953).

Langer, Susanne, *Problems of Art* (Routledge & Kegan Paul, 1957).

Layton, Robert, *Sibelius* (J. M. Dent, 1965).

Lewis, Peter, 'Wittgenstein on words and music', *Br. J. Aesthetics*, Vol. 17.

Mellers, Wilfrid, *Bach and the Dance of God* (Faber & Faber, 1980).

Morris-Jones, Huw, 'The language of feeling', *Br. J. Aesthetics*, Vol. 2.

Mounce, Howard, 'Art and real life', *Philosophy*, April (1980).

Newman, William, *The Sonata since Beethoven* (University of North Carolina Press, 1969).

Previn, André (with Antony Hopkins), *Music Face to Face* (Hamish Hamilton, 1971).

Rosen, Charles, *Sonata Forms* (W. W. Norton, 1980).

Scholes, Percy A., *The Listener's History of Music* (Oxford University Press, 1923).

Scruton, Roger, *Art and Imagination* (Methuen, 1974).

Shiner, Roger, 'Wittgenstein on the Beautiful, the Good and the Tremendous', *Br. J. Aesthetics*, Vol. 14 (1974).

Simpson, Robert, 'The chamber music for strings', in *The Beethoven Companion* (Faber & Faber, 1973).

Tovey, D. F., *Essays in Musical Analysis* (Oxford University Press, 1937).

Wagner, Richard, *A Happy Evening* (*Abend Zeitung*, Dresden, 1841).

Walker, Alan, *Franz Liszt: the Virtuoso Years* (Faber, 1983).

Winch, Peter, 'Text and context', *Philosophical Investigations*, Vol. 5 (1982).

Wisdom, John, *Paradox and Discovery* (Basil Blackwell, 1965).

Wittgenstein, Ludwig, *Culture and Value* (Basil Blackwell, 1980).

Wittgenstein, Ludwig, *Lectures and Conversations on Aesthetics, Psychology and Religious Belief* (Basil Blackwell, 1966).

Wittgenstein, Ludwig, *Philosophical Investigations* (Basil Blackwell, 1967).

Wittgenstein, Ludwig, *Zettel* (Basil Blackwell, 1967).

Wollheim, Richard, *Art and its Objects* (Penguin, 1975).

Index

Figures in **bold** refer to quotations from the author or work in question.